JAMES CLERK MAXWELL

JAMES
CLERK
MAXWELL

A Biography

IVAN TOLSTOY

CANONGATE
Edinburgh
1981

First published in 1981
by Canongate Publishing Ltd
17 Jeffrey Street, Edinburgh

ISBN 0 86241 010 X

The publishers acknowledge
the financial assistance of
the Scottish Arts Council in
the publication of this volume

Typeset by Hewer Text Composition Services, Edinburgh
Printed and bound by Butler & Tanner Ltd, Frome and London

CONTENTS

ACKNOWLEDGEMENTS

Many people have been most kind and helpful – providing me with information, steering me in appropriate directions and giving me their time. I would especially like to thank Professor Cyril Domb of King's College London, Professor L. C. Woods of Balliol College Oxford, Mr D. E. Muspratt of the Working Men's College in London, Professor T. G. Cowling and Dr John Brindley of Leeds University, Professor A. F. Brown of the City University of London, Sir John Clerk of Penicuik, Brigadier J. Wedderburn Maxwell, Mr Sam Callander of Parton, Mr John Thomson of Minnydow in Kirkpatrick Durham, Mr Larry Porteous of Knockvennie, and the Revd Andrew MacKay of the Manse, Kirkpatrick Durham. I have received valuable help from Canongate Publishing, notably from Mr Peter Chiene and Stephanie Wolfe Murray. I am also much in debt to my brother Professor D. Obolensky of Christ Church, Oxford, who found time to shepherd me through parts of the Oxbridge establishment, and to my wife Margie who has been a constant source of encouragement.

PREFACE

For physicists the name of James Clerk Maxwell ranks next to Newton and Einstein. Yet among non-scientific people Maxwell's image is surprisingly faint. It is hoped the present book will help remedy that injustice. This pretends neither to be a definitive biography, nor a work of historical scholarship. It is, rather, a book for the lay reader. Apart from a few oddments gleaned from the Maxwell collections at Cambridge, it contains little new or startling material. The emphasis, though, is different from other studies in that I have laid stress on Maxwell's *wholeness* – the remarkable way in which from an early age, his life, his work, and his philosophy were always interwoven.

In drawing a picture of the man I relied mostly on what historians call secondary sources. At the same time I have attempted to convey some feeling for Maxwell's qualities as a thinker by quoting, as much as possible, from his own writings.

A major source of information on Maxwell's life is Campbell and Garnett's very Victorian and hagiographic 1882 biography (which had a second edition in 1884; both are long out of print and difficult to find). While it represents the bulk of the available personal material, it is incomplete. More up-to-date studies of general interest by C. Domb, C. W. F. Everitt, L. C. Woods, J. G. Crowther, R. V. Jones, R. A. R. Tricker and

D. K. C. MacDonald contain additional material. Together with the 1931 centenary volume edited by J. J. Thomson, they fill out the picture – and underline some gaps.

The Campbell and Garnett book contains a summary of Maxwell's work by Garnett – his assistant at the Cavendish – illustrating, albeit unintentionally, how little the profound significance of his great work on electromagnetism was understood by his contemporaries. Neither Garnett, nor indeed most of Maxwell's more distinguished colleagues, ever grasped its revolutionary nature. In the 1931 commemorative volume, of course, with its homages by Einstein, Planck, Jeans and others, one sees his work universally and fully admired. Today, scholarly analyses of Maxwell's thinking are a growing industry – witness modern essays such as those of Everitt, Wise or Tricker.

Since this is not a technical book, I have been very selective in my choice of material – but so is any biographer who condenses a great man's life and work into a couple of hundred pages. To put Maxwell's major contributions into perspective I have introduced asides on the history of science, without which it seems impossible to appreciate the epochal and truly revolutionary nature of his work.

Ivan Tolstoy
Knockvennie
December 1980

1
A VICTORIAN GENIUS

Every so often someone revolutionizes a field of endeavour and thereby alters, irrevocably, our perception of the world. This requires a rare combination of insight, perseverance, talent and something more – a strange, magical touch, a kind of integrating faculty which transcends mere reason and defies analysis. The person who has this power and successfully applies it, we call a genius. Newton and Einstein were such men; and so too was Maxwell.

To call someone a genius implies that he or she is endowed with a peculiar gift, the workings of which we do not fully understand. It says little otherwise about the person; apart from a shared proclivity for altering the world, people of genius fit into no mould. The development of their talent, in particular, varies widely. Some, like Mozart, begin in child-hood – extracting, miraculously, fully made works of art from enigmatic, inner reservoirs of invention. Others, such as Einstein, are indifferent students and flower suddenly, with-out warning. Occasionally, as in Balzac's case, a genius serves a long apprenticeship turning out second-rate hack work. Some, like Darwin, develop steadily and publish their *magnum opus* as mature men in their forties or fifties. Gauss, the prince of mathematicians, produced much of his best work as a young man in his teens and early twenties. Maxwell compromised; he showed early signs of promise, did his most brilliant thinking between the ages of twenty-nine and thirty-five, and published several masterpieces when he was past forty.

Shy, retiring, eccentric, Maxwell's public image has always been faint. He was, one might say, a genius who never made good copy. Certainly his name is not so widely known as Newton's or Einstein's; yet his contribution to science has been of the same order. He was, and largely remains to this day, a physicist's physicist – appreciated and revered by those equipped to understand and savour his work at first hand. *Their* praise, always, has been superlative and unstinting. Einstein, discussing Maxwell's discovery of the laws of electrodynamics, said: 'To few men in the world has such an experience been vouchsafed.' The normally staid *Encyclopaedia Britannica* (1954), in an article written by P. G. Tait – a contemporary and one of the grand old men of Victorian physics – described Maxwell's formulation of these laws as 'One of the most splendid monuments ever raised by the genius of a single individual'. Richard Feynman of Caltech, a star physicist himself, once stated that in the far future 'the most significant event of the nineteenth century will be judged as Maxwell's discovery of the laws of electrodynamics. The American Civil War will pale into provincial insignificance in comparison with this important scientific event of the same decade.' In a later chapter I will try to show why such statements cannot be dismissed as mere hyperbole.

Like Newton, Maxwell was an unusual combination of mathematician and experimenter – a theoretical physicist with a thorough understanding of laboratory technique and a magnificent intuition. He contributed significantly to the analysis of colour perception, to an explanation of Saturn's rings, to the theory of fluids and solids. He and Boltzmann fathered modern statistical mechanics and the molecular theory of gases. For this alone, Maxwell would have been recognized as a foremost physicist of his era. But his greatest work, which put him in a class apart amongst the immortals of science, was the theory of electromagnetism – the formulation of the equations, or laws, that bear his name.

No great discovery is ever the exclusive creation of one person. Newton once said that he achieved what he did because he had stood on the shoulders of giants. Einstein could not have formulated relativity without Maxwell's equations. Maxwell's work was likewise the culmination of a long line of electrical and magnetic researches.

Two thousand six hundred years ago, Thales of Miletus had studied the lodestone – magnetized bits of iron ore which attracted and repelled each other in odd, seemingly inexplicable ways. Observations of static electricity are also ancient, probably dating from before the Greeks. Ultimate manifestations of the subatomic world, these were subtle matters – how much so only became apparent in modern times; electricity and magnetism, we now know, are fundamental properties, the basic stuff of the universe, as basic as mass, and perhaps like it involving the very fabric of space and time. It is hardly surprising, therefore, that understanding developed slowly. As late as the sixteenth century mankind's knowledge of these matters was largely lore – a collection of curious facts about rubbed pieces of amber, the odd behaviour of the lodestone or the marine compass. William Gilbert, for instance, the great Elizabethan man of science, held that magnets possessed a strange, spiritual essence, and that the Earth's magnetism was also its soul.

Necessary for the development of the modern picture of electromagnetism were later advances, such as the battery (1800), allowing one to produce and control the flow of electricity. It was found then that electric currents generated magnetism. In France Ampère gave a rule for calculating the magnetic forces due to a current: he was one of the giants on whose shoulders Maxwell stood. Another was Faraday, the self-taught blacksmith's son, who first conceived the idea of *field*. Noting the pattern assumed by iron filings near a magnet, he concluded that they gave a picture of the actual direction of the forces acting on them – the lines of force. Faraday had the brilliant notion that all electric and magnetic forces were distributed this way, in well-defined geometrical patterns, through all of space. This intuition was the basis of the idea of force field and of the whole field concept, so central in modern physics. Faraday further proved that a changing magnetic field produced a current of an electrical conductor: this was magnetic induction, the principle of the dynamo.

Faraday's and Ampère's work was fundamental – it provided the link between electricity and magnetism. The two kinds of force were henceforth unified under a single concept: the electromagnetic field. It was the beginning of the grand synthesis.

James Clerk Maxwell completed the picture and put the theory in its modern form: he combined the laws of electromagnetism into a simple, lucid mathematical statement – a set of famous relations known as Maxwell's equations. These provided the theoretical foundation of modern electromagnetic science – the basis of much, if not most, of our technological civilization. But what Maxwell created was far more than a mathematical restatement of other men's discoveries or the seeds of a technological revolution. What he offered was a completely new outlook, replacing the Newtonian universe of particles and action-at-a-distance forces by a world of fields, an abstract world beyond the ken of our senses. It was a true *scientific revolution*, and it signalled the birth of modern physics.

While Maxwell lived, and for some years thereafter, his theory of electricity and magnetism was appreciated only by a small scientific élite. Its deeper implications were not fully understood until long after his death. The book which summarized it, the *Treatise on Electricity and Magnetism*, is beyond the reach of many – largely on account of its mathematical form. Yet this does not wholly explain Maxwell's lack of public lustre. Einstein's work, after all, was equally esoteric – if not more so – yet he was, during his lifetime, a celebrated and newsworthy figure. Part of the explanation lies in that the times were very different. In Maxwell's day science, as a profession, had yet to have urged upon it the attentions of the media – or its temptations of instant celebrity. Another reason was Maxwell's indifference to fame; even by the restrained standards of his contemporaries, he was a modest and retiring man.

Personal descriptions of Maxwell come to us from recorded comments of colleagues and friends. Most of this information can be gathered from one source: a biography written by his life-long friend, the Reverend Lewis Campbell. Published in 1882 and long out of print, it contains a solid store of facts, letters, and anecdotes. It is also hagiographic and unfortunately confronts us with many a discreet omission. It is particularly detailed in its description of Maxwell as a boy and as a student. At this stage at least, Campbell makes it clear that he was an odd and eccentric young man. Indeed, he states that when Maxwell entered the University of Edinburgh he 'still occasioned some concern to the more conventional amongst his friends by the originality and simplicity of his ways'. Campbell further reports that when ill at ease Maxwell could lapse into 'chaotic statements' – an impediment he kept until the end of his days. But, while Campbell's biography is a godsend to all students of Maxwell's life, it is incomplete. It offers no description of his wife – a person said by some to have been difficult and perhaps neurotic. And it makes no mention of his first love for his cousin Elizabeth Cay – a relationship unearthed not long ago by C. W. F. Everitt.

Nevertheless Campbell supplies us with valuable insight into Maxwell's religious views and philosophy of life – which appear to have been basic and simple, almost incongruously so. That he had a social conscience is shown by his interest in teaching working men. Yet he demonstrated little, if any, inclination to rebel – against family, society or church. Interested in the technical problems of his day, he still never ventured into the world of industrial science. J. G. Crowther has called him a feudalist, with a feudal sense of duty which made him devote time to tasks quite unrelated to his scientific interests. Family and friends were important to him; at times they took precedence over all else. In this one might again contrast him to Newton, whose single-minded, compulsive intellectual activity was almost demonic, or to Einstein who, while he had a powerful social conscience and gave much time to causes, considered personal commitments as impediments to his life's work. Maxwell wrote a certain amount of verse; as poetry it may not be very good, but the poems reveal aspects of his personality he was otherwise too shy to display. Several, written in times of sadness or stress, are touching and show us a gentle and sensitive man.

After holding professorships at Aberdeen and London, Maxwell went into apparent semi-retirement between 1865 and 1871. During this period he held no academic post, lived on his Glenlair estate, tended to his duties as the local laird, rode horseback, wrote a large number of scientific papers, much of his *Treatise on Electricity and Magnetism* and, in the evenings, read poetry and Shakespeare with his wife. His colleagues thought him peculiar; he was what we would call today *a character* – original, strong-minded and independent yet at the same time strangely shy and quite lacking in presumption. One of his last great efforts was the editing at Cambridge of Henry Cavendish's unpublished researches on electricity – a striking example of his self-effacement and sense of duty. Many have felt, as I do, that this substantial effort may have been better directed by Maxwell into pursuing his own, deeper insights into these matters. Perhaps so. Yet there may be in such judgements a tinge of impertinence. Creativity is a wayward, exotic flower; none can tell how it prospers, nor why it dies.

When assessing Maxwell as a man one must keep in mind how different from ours was the spirit of his times. For us who practice science in the latter half of the twentieth century, it can be an effort to see the pursuit of knowledge as Maxwell saw it –

as a vocation. If one were ambitious *and* possessed of a truly brilliant scientific mind one could like W. Thomson – later Lord Kelvin – achieve fame and riches. But on the whole science in the nineteenth century was an unglamorous profession – if, indeed, one could have called it a profession at all. Remuneration was not generous; Faraday's salary at the Royal Institution, at the peak of his fame, was 'a hundred pounds per annum, house, coal and candles'; Maxwell's, at Cambridge, was five hundred pounds. The effects of such lack of munificence were not entirely bad, however. Careerism in the sciences was unknown, as were the power structures of Big Science. Except for an occasional squabble over priorities, science in the nineteenth century was a reasonably honourable and dignified affair. Yet even against this temperate, low-key backdrop Maxwell seems to have been singularly modest, reticent and detached. This is probably why he received relatively few honours during his lifetime; he simply didn't care. The cynic might remark that Maxwell could afford to be aloof; he was comfortably off; and if his ideas were not wholly accepted, his brilliance was still recognized and assured him of a hearing in the most distinguished circles of his profession – of which, of course, he was himself a prominent member. No doubt this did contribute to an equable outlook and a degree of detachment. But it explains neither his seeming indifference to fame nor his genuine lack of arrogance. These I think were true reflections of the inner man, a man of integrity and one who, both in his scientific and everyday philosophies, was something of a mystic – an unworldly, strange and thoroughly interesting man.

2

A CURIOUS CHILD

In the late afternoon of 29 August 1831 in a poorly lit room of London's Royal Institution, a man bent over a table. He was about forty, clean-shaven, with a full humorous mouth and strong, open, regular features. On the scratched and stained oak surface before him lay a ring-shaped contraption wrapped in calico and twine, with thin copper wires emerging at various angles; two of these snaked over towards a battery – a cumbersome thing of stacked plates and damp layers of cloth standing in a corner; another pair was bent into a closed, solitary coil mounted about a small needle compass about three feet away.

The man's expression was rapt – a mixture of total concentration and controlled triumph: after years of thought, frustration and painstaking work, Michael Faraday had finally observed magnetic induction. Several times now, after closing and opening a switch, he had seen the needle tremble and waver: a changing magnetic field in his ring-wound coils had generated a surge of current – which in turn had created its own magnetic field in the solitary coil and deflected the compass. He had completed the cycle begun by Ørsted the Dane who in 1820 had shown (by accident, it was said) that an electric current in a wire gave rise to magnetic forces – an effect quickly verified and elaborated by Ampère in France.

There was nothing accidental about Faraday's discovery. The human mind has a penchant for symmetry and after Ørsted it had occurred to many that the converse could be true: magnetic fields might likewise generate electric currents. A number of people had tried to demonstrate this. But Faraday, with his physical insight and endless perseverance, was the first to succeed. On this late summer afternoon of 1831 he had with unerring instinct put his finger on the point that others had missed: to induce a current in a wire, the magnetic field had to be *changing* – *that* was the secret of magnetic induction. A changing magnetic flux would generate a current, just as a current would give rise to a magnetic field. Man's view of the universe would henceforth have to include this mutual embrace of electric and magnetic forces – reciprocal, symmetric manifestations of one basic phenomenon, soon to be named the electromagnetic field.

As he put it to a friend later, Faraday was not yet certain whether it was a weed or a fish he had at last pulled up. It took him three months to carry out more observations, to tie up loose ends, to pin down the phenomenon. And then there was no doubt, no doubt at all he had made a momentous discovery – perhaps the greatest in his life, and one which would eventually completely alter man's view of the cosmos. Faraday also guessed that it would someday change the face of industry and with it the world. This, after all, was the principle of the dynamo – a principle which would allow mankind to generate almost unlimited quantities of electricity from huge, oddly shaped, spinning blocks of iron weighing many tons, machined to clearances of a sixteenth of an inch, driven at dizzy speeds by torrents of water inside great dams or by steam turbines housed in vast power stations – energy for whole cities and countries, power for a technological revolution the likes of which had never been seen before. The real scale of things to come no doubt eluded him; but he must at least have glimpsed the broad, long-term implications of his discovery. Yet for this Faraday cared little. He was to turn down several offers of lucrative consulting jobs. His life, he decided, would be chiefly devoted to refining his picture of electricity and magnetism, to formulating a body of accurate and unexceptionable knowledge for others to work with – others, perhaps greater than himself, who would come after and sooner or later make of his discoveries a rigorous, universal body of theory. It all stemmed from the trembling of a compass needle, observed on that summer afternoon in 1831.

★   ★   ★

At the same time in Edinburgh, in a comfortable three-storey house in India Street, an infant was making acquaintance with the world – watching, as infants must, strange beings and incomprehensible shapes moving in and out of the field of vision, clenching fists, crying, kicking, being picked up, washed, changed, cuddled, subjected to a rich assortment of noises, smells, hues, lights and shadows – an exciting, interesting world, a world of infinite variety and riches. James Clerk Maxwell was born in that same summer of 1831, a few months before Faraday made his celebrated discovery.

Unlike Faraday, whose father was a Yorkshire blacksmith, Maxwell came of landed gentry, its lines extending back to the days of Mary, Queen of Scots. He was descended from the Clerks of Penicuik, who had been forced to leave Aberdeenshire in 1568 on account of their loyalty to Queen Mary. The family fortunes had waxed and waned through the centuries. His ancestry, however, was always privileged, civilized, and occasionally unconventional. Family friendships included people like Sir Robert Peel and Walter Scott. A great uncle had been a friend and collaborator of James Hutton, whose *Theory of the Earth* had in 1785 marked the birth of modern geology. An earlier forebear, Sir John Clerk, an accomplished musician, had served in the Parliament of Scotland and is said to have fought off sixteen robbers who in 1762 had attacked his house in Penicuik. A grandfather, James Clerk, was a captain in the East Indian navy. It is told of him that when his ship was wrecked on the coast of India, he swam to land using the bag of his pipes as a float; having clambered ashore he began to play the bagpipes uncommonly loud ('an unco fit'), thereby cheering the survivors *and* keeping the Bengal tigers at bay – an authentic story, it seems, repeated with relish by the family whenever occasion arose. The younger of the captain's two sons, John, inherited the Galloway estate of Middlebie, which had come into the family through marriage to a Maxwell, and added Maxwell to his name.

John Clerk Maxwell, as he then became, was by profession an Edinburgh lawyer; his practice, apparently, was desultory. He seems to have been benign, intelligent, idiosyncratic and somewhat ineffectual. After the death of his mother, with whom he had been living, he married Frances Cay of Charlton, Northumberland. It was for both a late marriage – he was thirty-nine, she was thirty-four. Intelligent, articulate and perhaps more enterprising than her husband, she spurred him into doing something with his Middlebie estate. A manor, largely designed by him, was eventually built and named Glenlair.

Their first child, a daughter, did not survive. Had today's statistics on the dangers of late parenthood been available to the Clerk Maxwells they might well have drawn the rational conclusion and desisted. Luckily they did not, and James Clerk Maxwell was born on 13 June 1831, the only child of middle-aged parents.

James' early childhood was spent at Glenlair. Galloway is a region of ancient Palaeozoic rock, rugged coasts, fertile valleys, steep fells and quiet lochs set amidst slate and granite mountains. The coastal hills, scoured by ice-age glaciers into smooth, rolling waves of earth and stone, are a complex chequerboard of dark copses, green and yellow fields, and pastures divided by dry-stone walls – the labour of generations. The pastures are sloping, at times precipitous, dotted with sheep – white spots on green baize – and the walls snake their way over the hills. Near the village of Knockvennie, on

11

an eminence between two burns – the Urr and the Lair – the house was built. It was a well-chosen spot, sheltered, facing southward down the opening valley. The climate here is tempered by the ocean and the Solway Firth. The winters, while blustery, are not harsh. The summer days are long and, in good years, full of gentle warmth and light breezes. In autumn the barley fields turn a golden brown and the hillside heather is mauve.

Maxwell's earliest memories were of sunlight. He remembered lying on his back in the grass at Glenlair, staring at the sky, watching the sun, observing its brilliance become tolerable as it hid behind a cloud, noting the perfect roundness of its disk, thinking how it then resembled the moon, and wondering – wondering how it worked and whether God had made it (his mother always told him God had made everything). He was two when the sun gave him his first thrill of independent experimentation: he discovered mirrors – in the form of a tin plate. He first thought he had captured the sun and summoned his parents to witness the miracle: a brilliant spot of light he could make dance at will upon the walls and ceiling of his room. 'It's the sun!' he cried. 'I got it with the tin plate!'

Before the age of three Maxwell already showed an exuberant curiosity. His mother, in a letter to her sister Jane Cay, dated April 1834 describes his activities in these terms:

> He is a very happy man, and has improved much since the weather got moderate; he has great work with doors, locks, keys, etc., and 'Show me how it doos' is never out of his mouth. He also investigates the hidden course of streams and bell-wires, the way the water gets from the pond through the wall and a pend or small bridge and down a drain into Water Orr, then past the smiddy and down to the sea, where Maggie's ships sail. As to the bells, they will not rust; he stands sentry in the kitchen, and Mag runs thro' the house ringing them all by turns, or he rings, and sends Bessy to see and shout to let him know, and he drags papa all over to show him the holes where the wires go through.

The Galloway air is pure and on clear frosty nights the heavens are open and crystalline, ablaze with stars, and the

Milky Way stretches from horizon to horizon. In the 1830s astronomers already knew that the stars are suns like ours, only immeasurably more distant, and the Milky Way an arm of the galaxy to which we belong. Telescopes had found, scattered in the far reaches of space, uncharted and uncounted, vast numbers of other galaxies. John Clerk Maxwell, who kept abreast of scientific notions, would on clear nights take his son outside stargazing and doubtless told him all this. One may imagine, then, on a winter evening, the small boy staring at the sky – as we all do at times – awe-struck by the immensity of space and the uncountable distant worlds. We can, alas, only speculate about the thoughts that must then have crossed his mind. But we know that many years later as a Cambridge student, he agreed with the poet Edward Young that 'an undevout astronomer is mad'.

All children are born with a sense of wonder and a profound inquisitiveness. Perhaps those destined for greatness have an unusual amount thereof, or perhaps, as they grow, they succeed – through circumstance or innate strength – in hanging on to a bigger share than most; one does not really know. Young Maxwell it is certain, had extraordinary supplies of curiosity. Apart from wishing to know how everything worked, or wondering about the sun, or trying to capture it in mirrors, he used to drag relatives, nurses, or other adults at hand, on endless walks through the glens, following torrent beds, or along the rock and bracken ridges of Mochrum, the High Craigs of Glenlair, or Bardarroch Hill. He came home with wildflowers, grasses, beetles, frogs, rock specimens – those myriad items adults so take for granted, but which the childish mind finds so deliciously interesting. In his collection there were, no doubt, gifts from his elders. His father, an amateur geologist in his youth, would have given him mineral specimens from far away places – perhaps a sparkling crystal of quartz, or a piece of Iceland spar with its strange trick of making things look double. He was much taken also by a scientific toy consisting of a spinning cylinder with a simple arrangement of holes which enabled figures drawn on the inside to acquire the appearance of movement – the so-called 'magic disk' or 'wheel of life'. He played with intricate colour arrangements and delighted in the shifting hues and colours of the magic disk.

James had a non-stop mind, boundless energy, and an outstanding memory – by the age of eight, he could recite the whole of the 119th psalm. He pestered everyone around him with questions: 'What's the go o'that?', 'What does it do?' With rather more pride than pique, his Aunt Jane complained once that 'it was humiliating to be asked so many questions one couldn't answer by a child like that'. The Maxwells clearly worshipped their son. The freedom, love, and attention they lavished upon him did much to encourage his curiosity and sense of wonder. Those early years must have been idyllic.

But the bliss of childhood is ever short-lived, even under the best of circumstances. When James was seven, it became obvious that his mother was seriously ill, probably with cancer. In a desperate effort to save her life, an operation was performed; this was before the age of anaesthetics, and she suffered dreadful agony. She died in December 1839. When told of her death, James exclaimed: 'Oh I'm so glad! Now she'll have no more pain!'

In Victorian times the rearing of children was largely the woman's business. Nevertheless, John Clerk Maxwell undertook the education of his small son conscientiously and with love (curiously, another important figure of nineteenth-century science, a fellow-Scotsman whom James was to know well – William Thomson, later Lord Kelvin – was likewise brought up by a widowed father). Mr Maxwell was much helped by his sister-in-law, Jane Cay, who became a pivotal figure of James' youth. She frequently visited Glenlair and in later years had James stay with her in Edinburgh. She was no doubt the classic spinster aunt – the unsung heroine of so many childhoods – lavishing love and attention upon the boy. Lewis Campbell, James' life-long friend, describes her as 'one of the warmest hearted creatures in the world, somewhat wayward in her likes and dislikes, perhaps warm-tempered also, but boundless in affectionate kindness to those whom she loved'.

James, of course, became enormously attached to Aunt Jane and to his father. With the latter, he developed a healthy, unsentimental friendship, following him about the estate, curious, helpful and energetically cheerful. Maxwell senior was a kind, decent, endlessly patient man. He was not always effectual but nevertheless did much to steer the boy's interests in the direction they took – if only by the example of his own enthusiasms, which ran to industrial machinery, technology and design. Yet in bringing up his son he committed some serious blunders.

The first was in his choice of tutor, hired after his wife's death. We have no adequate description of the man – merely an incidental, rather humorous drawing by a cousin, Jemima Wedderburn, showing young James floating on a pond in a washtub, determinedly paddling away from a large man in a stovepipe hat. This is the tutor – a snub nose, thick lips and a grim expression give him an ungentle, lumpish air. With a garden rake, he is trying, unsuccessfully, to hook onto James' vessel. Standing about in various attitudes of fascination is an assortment of relatives and playmates. Aunt Jane is there; so is James' father; *his* expression is one of benign amusement.

The tutor was rough on the boy. He believed obviously that to make young lads behave and absorb learning, they had to be coerced – physically, when necessary. This educational philosophy found no answering chord in his pupil. Quite likely the man was himself badgered and at times harassed, and had his patience strained on more than one occasion. We have no account of actual instances of provocation of the tutor, but there is one authentic story of James' general inventiveness and propensity for raising the devil. One winter night, when his father's parlour maid was about to enter the dining room with a full tray, the boy quickly blew out the candles and lay down on the floor across the doorway. Subsequent details are unavailable, but they must have been satisfyingly horrendous.

James was the product of a humane and, for those times, remarkably permissive upbringing; by Victorian standards, he must have seemed spoilt and headstrong. The tutor, we may surmise, had his hands full. Nevertheless, one feels little sympathy for a teacher who tries to instil spelling and arithmetic by beating his small charge over the head with a ruler and twisting his ears until they bled. Like many an incompetent pedagogue before and since, he tried to blame the child – claiming that James was slow and wayward. Curiously, it took Mr Clerk Maxwell and Jane Cay almost two years to discover what was going on. J. G. Crowther has suggested that James could not bring himself to complain of mistreatment by a social inferior; the British were – and still are – a class-conscious people, and the Scots are no exception; this is a plausible theory. It seems likely, though, that such violence was infrequent, or it would have been discovered sooner. James, knowing well that local boys with whom he played – like Sandy Fraser or Sam Murdoch – were as a matter of course treated this way at school may have simply decided that the manly thing to do was to stick it out. Be that as it may, he was a sensitive boy and the episode must have left long-lasting scars. Some strange mannerisms and a lasting speech difficulty may have dated from that period. Music also caused him ear pains until he was past sixteen – a possible result of all the ear-pulling. The heavy-handed pedagogue, who knew no better and who must himself have been taught by such methods, was sacked.

Considerable soul-searching ensued and it was decided to send James to a day school in Edinburgh – the Edinburgh Academy, patronized by the Scottish professional élite. It was arranged that he would stay with an aunt – Mrs Wedderburn, his father's widowed sister. Mr Clerk Maxwell himself would continue at Glenlair, and come up for frequent visits.

The move took place in mid-November 1841. Edinburgh is

about ninety miles north-east of Glenlair. Today by car on well-surfaced roads the trip takes two or two and a half hours. But a hundred and forty years ago in coach and horses using dirt roads, a leisurely journey required two days, with a stop-over for the night. The way is through sparsely settled regions, mountainous, heather and bracken-covered, wild; James must have found it all hugely exciting and delightful. The Maxwells made a slow voyage, stopping with cousins, first in Newton, then in Penicuik. Familiar faces, family yarns, the warmth of roaring fires on frosty autumn nights – all, one may be sure, contributed to the voyage's enjoyment. They arrived at dusk on 18 November, at 31 Heriot Row, amidst a welter of welcoming relatives, servants, luggage, and a few spectators. Henceforth this handsome, solid four-storey town house in one of Edinburgh's most affluent sections – Old 31, as it would be referred to in the family – would be young Maxwell's home during the school terms.

The idea of the Edinburgh Academy was conceived by a liberal minded group of people including some eminent Edinburgh men who had found the Royal High School sadly inadequate. The founders were Henry Cockburn, John Russel and Leonard Horner. Sir Walter Scott became one of its subscribers and opened the school at the official ceremony in 1824. In its day a model of enlightenment, it was to be the focus of James' education for the next six years. It still stands almost unchanged in the heart of Edinburgh, within easy walking distance of Heriot Row. The classrooms are laid out in low, ground-level buildings around a good-sized yard. On the frieze of the central colonnaded edifice are the inevitable classical aphorisms. Grey, severe, this institution is the embodiment in stone of nineteenth century education.

But unlike many British public schools of its day it gave the older students a good background in mathematics and some understanding of physics. It also instilled a powerful and traditional dose of Latin and Greek; by the age of twelve the boys could conjugate 800 irregular Greek verbs. One can debate endlessly how much a child does or does not profit from this kind of institutionalized intellectual violence; such arguments tend to illuminate little save the debater's prejudices. That it did no permanent harm to Maxwell's great talent seems undeniable; yet this could be a compliment to him rather than to the system. The first years at the Academy were painful ones.

Once again, in inaugurating a new chapter in James' life the father showed a strange lack of acumen, thereby causing his son much anguish. John Clerk Maxwell, it must be emphasized, was a genuinely decent, concerned parent, who dearly loved his boy and took great pains to ensure a good education. However, he had his vagaries – eccentricities which, as is often the case, bespoke of a strong confidence in his own judgement and occasionally of a healthy disregard for the opinions of others. He had, for instance, a truly artistocratic indifference to appearances and one of his pet idiosyncrasies was that he liked, as much as possible, to design the objects that he used – from the shoes he wore to the houses he lived in. Among other things, he had designed James' square-toed boots with their bronze clasps and his hodden grey tweed tunic. Both were eminently practical for life in Galloway, but had little in common with schoolboy fashion, which ran to narrower shoes with black tape, and round jackets. For his first day at school a frilly collar was added – a touch of gentility due probably to his aunt.

By nature or nurture, schoolchildren are, all too often, caricatures of their elders. Prominent amongst their social vices – encouraged by their schooling – is a kind of desperate conformism which, when threatened, stops at little in trying to force things back into an accepted framework. So when young Maxwell showed up at the Academy in his country clothes, his schoolmates set upon him with zest. They ripped off his collar, mussed his carefully brushed hair, tore his shirt, sniggered at his shoes, laughed at his efforts to defend himself and, generally speaking, had an uproarious time at his expense.

As in the tutor episode, James demonstrated a deep-seated toughness. He stood his ground as best he could, tried sarcasm – a wasted effort which merely impressed his tormentors as freakish – and attempted to resist physically. He was a gentle soul, though, and of course got the worst of it. Yet he resisted the temptation to complain and exact retribution through his teachers and gave, when he came home to 31 Heriot Row, a convincing display of amusement at the barbaric behaviour of his classmates.

They persecuted him for years. Occasionally he turned upon the little ruffians and defended himself with a kind of furious strength which took them by surprise and earned him periods of respite. Once he was helped by Lewis Campbell who, thereafter, became his life-long friend and eventual biographer. Slowly over the years James won the grudging respect of his classmates. However, with the exception of Campbell and one or two later friends, they always looked at him with suspicion. He was simply too different. No doubt his family acquired for him, soon enough, more conventional clothing. But in other respects he remained uncompromisingly himself. What could a lot of game-loving, study-hating, rambunctious, middle-class boys think of one who spent his spare time reading, collecting strange things, doing experiments with odd bits of scrap? One who in addition was small for his age, spouted odd sayings with a Galloway brogue and stuttered to boot? He was obviously a daft one and accordingly they nicknamed him 'Dafty' – a name that stuck through six years of school.

In his first years at the Academy, this brilliant boy was a poor scholar – a reflection both of his private misery and the system of schooling. His speech difficulties for a while grew worse and provided his fellow students with a further instrument of torture. Eventually, James coped with this too; he learned to combat his stutter by memorizing lessons copied onto a sketch of his classroom window: seeing the window would act as a jog to his memory and he could then recite the lesson faultlessly. We can only guess at the effects of those early years; of one thing, however, we can be sure: James Clerk Maxwell was not a happy schoolboy. One finds no written record of how he felt about his tormentors. Only as a grown man, recalling his school years, he was to say with a thin, sad smile: 'They never understood me; but I understood them'.

After three years or so he had weathered the worst. He acquired then a form of self-expression he was to use for the rest of his life. He developed a facility for versifying and henceforth, whenever he had something important or private to say, he would write a poem – to be circulated amongst interested parties or to be slipped quietly, without comment, to some particular friend. Here is a sample written at the age of thirteen, in which reference is made to the brutal schooling and to both the classics teacher (Carmichael) and the rector (Archdeacon Williams); it displays a gentle humour and a fine sense of irony:

> Ne'er shall the dreadful tawse be heard again,
> The lash resounding, and the cry of pain;
> Carmichael's self will change (O that he would!)
> From the imperative to the wishing mood;
> Ye years roll on, and haste the expected time
> When flogging boys shall be accounted crime
>
> But come, thy real nature let us see.
> No more the rector but the godess be,
> Come in thy might and shake the deep profound,
> Let the Academy with shouts resound,
> While radiant glory all thy head adorns
> And slippers on thy feet protect thy corns;
> O may I live so long on earth below
> That I may learn the things that thou dost know

Edinburgh was an unhealthy place, especially in the winters when there hung everywhere the stench of coal smoke; the city was referred to in those days as Auld Reekie. Living there did little for Maxwell's health; he had more than his share of colds and coughs. Except for the holidays, which he spent at Glenlair, his life was centered at Old 31. His frequent, chatty letters to his father show that, despite his tribulations at school, his mind was bright, growing, and far ahead of his peers. The gentility of Maxwell's family upbringing and his sensitivity should not delude us: James was mentally tough and resilient – a *survivor* who would not be broken by a gang of boys or a Victorian Academy.

School and voracious reading already took up much of young Maxwell's life. He dabbled promisingly in art – showing among other things a taste for design. He grew close with his relatives – his numerous Cay cousins, aunts, and uncles who provided him with warm and friendly family relationships. In April 1842 he writes to Glenlair:

> My Dear Papa, The day you went away Lizzy and I went to the Zoological Gardens, and they have got an elephant, and Lizzy was frightened for its ugly face.

Lizzy – Cousin Elizabeth – then a child of two, was one he would grow particularly fond of as the years went by. In March 1844, in a letter which already sounds more grown up, she is mentioned again:

> My Dear Father, On Saturday last we went to the Marine Villa . . . I found where shellfish breed; they breed in sea syke; there were muscles, cocles and oysters no bigger than these . . . fastened to the syke by filaments . . . Lizzy says when you come back it would not be displeasing to her if you would bring a bawl of grey worsted.

The misspellings, one suspects, are deliberate – perhaps a private joke between himself and Mr Maxwell.

The high points of those early years in Edinburgh were his father's visits and their occasional Saturday walks. They viewed together the building of the Granton railway, the stratification of the Salisbury Crags, Leith Port, and other places. Those were the years when the technological potential of electro-magnetism was stirring – even though the subject was, scientifically speaking, poorly understood. By 1835 Joseph Henry in America had invented the first electric motor. Robert Davidson of Aberdeen had in 1838 finished a five ton electric locomotive which made several trips on the Glasgow-Edinburgh railway. And on one winter Saturday in 1842, the Maxwells went to see some 'electro-magnetic machines' – early applications of the self-same principles of induction Faraday had uncovered and which James would one day cast in universal mathematical form and master as no man had before.

18 December 1843 was an interesting date: father took son to a meeting of the Edinburgh Royal Society. At the age of twelve James Clerk Maxwell attended his first scientific meeting. His impressions of that occasion have not been re-corded and we can only speculate on its importance for his development. Mr Maxwell was, at the very least, intent on encouraging his son's curiosity; and clearly the boy was to have every educational advantage his father could conceive.

The Maxwells were well acquainted with Professor James Thomson, then professor of mathematics at the University of Glasgow, and his gifted sons William and James. The latter would end up as professor of engineering in Glasgow. In 1846 William, at the age of twenty-two, secured the chair of natural philosophy at this university. William was a true *Wunderkind*; he had matriculated at the university at the age of twelve and would become the most renowned and honoured British physicist of his time (he received a peerage in his later years and became Lord Kelvin of Largs). Young Maxwell was to spend time during the holidays with the Thomsons – absorbing, one may be sure, the atmosphere of scientific curiosity and knowledge which pervaded this remarkable household.

A milestone, recorded in a letter from James to his father, was reached in June 1844, when he announced: 'I have made a tetrahedron, a dodecahedron, and two other hedrons whose names I don't know'. Without prior instruction in geometry, young Maxwell had discovered for himself and constructed models of the regular polyhedra: the first stirrings of a fledgling mathematician.

His chief sources of happiness remained at Glenlair. The long summer days, the heather and bracken-covered hills, the sparkling burns, the rolling pastures gave the bright, sensitive boy the resources he needed to cope with the vagaries of teachers, schoolmates, and the Edinburgh winters. Throughout his life he was to love this place above all others and return to it to replenish his reserves of strength, sanity, and health. It was ever to be a cornerstone of his existence.

3

STIRRINGS OF GREATNESS

Of all western sciences geometry was first to mature. Like so much of our knowledge, it sprang from ancient, practical roots – the need in Sumer, Babylon and Egypt to measure distances, areas and volumes. The Greeks, with their talent for abstract thinking, formalized the subject, turning it into a branch of mathematics; and because Euclid systematically garnered, developed and expounded the principles and theorems upon which this knowledge rested, it became known as Euclidean geometry. Its austere perfection has intrigued many minds. As adolescents Einstein, Russell, Pascal and others were deeply affected by its vision. Even non-mathematicians find themselves bewitched; the poet, Edna St Vincent Millay, put it this way: 'Euclid alone has looked on Beauty bare'. There is in geometry an almost therapeutic quality; it offers truth in a world where certainty is rare – a framework and a set of rules which, if followed faithfully, lead to conclusions that are invariably and certifiably true.

Maxwell was captivated by geometry at an early age. His spontaneous rediscovery of the regular polyhedra, before he had received any formal instruction, is proof enough of an early enthralment, of his intuitive understanding of the properties of space. This intuition, which allowed him to perceive essential relationships with ease, would characterize all his work as a scientist; it was perhaps the most remarkable of his talents. Maxwell's celebrated physical insight was, one suspects, just that: an acute geometrical vision, which permitted his mind's eye to see with exceptional clarity the interplay in space of figures and motion. It is a rare gift.

When at the age of thirteen Maxwell entered the Academy's fifth form and began the formal study of geometry, his school life was transformed. The teacher, Mr Gloag, was a gruff and acerbic character – 'Ha booy! Are ye making baskets wi' your legs?' he railed at some hapless boy wriggling desperately in his seat. He was a good instructor, though, respected by his students, and spurred many to new efforts, C. G. Knott, an applied mathematician of some distinction and also a pupil of his, described him as 'a teacher of strenuous character and quaint originality'. After years of indifferent performance Maxwell blossomed and received in 1845 the school's mathematical medal, the first prize for English and for English Verse. His erstwhile tormentors now gave him a kind of grudging, puzzled respect; there was more than met the eye to this odd, stuttering boy. But he remained a loner and made friends with only a few boys – like Lewis Campbell, who would eventually join the ministry and became a renowned classicist, or P. G. Tait, who was to be a very fine physicist himself.

Mr Clerk Maxwell, much gratified by his son's progress at school, began shepherding him regularly to meetings of the Royal Society of Edinburgh. Within this one year, James had not only turned into a brilliant student but had also begun his life-long immersion in scientific inquiry.

The results were immediate and startling: at the age of fourteen, in February 1846, he completed his first piece of original research, on some problems of geometry. It involved a discussion of ovals – generalizations of the ellipse. The Greeks, of course, had discovered a great deal about the latter – a curve defined by two fixed points, or foci: the sum of their distances to any point of the ellipse is constant. Young Maxwell investigated the case for which multiples of these distances add up to a constant. He also examined curves with more than two foci. Most remarkable in this work was not its skill, but the fact that it had occurred, to a boy of fourteen, to generalize in this way the theory of the ellipse. Here, in the earliest of his published works, is evidence of one of Maxwell's outstanding talents: an ability and willingness to generalize. Such generalizations are characteristic of much that is best in scientific and mathematical research. Evident in this study is his desire to stay in touch with practicalities: he proposed ingenious arrangements of pins and strings for constructing these ovals. Maxwell's intuition was never formal – he did not work happily with abstract mathematical themes. Geometry, on the other hand, suited him well; the spatial relationships with which it deals are not abstract, and their visualization requires the kind of intuition at which Maxwell excelled.

The boy's obvious enthusiasm at his discoveries communicated itself to his father, who took the manuscript to Professor James Forbes of the University of Edinburgh, a physicist, mountaineer, and glaciologist of distinction, author of *The Theory of Glaciers*. After consulting a mathematical colleague, Forbes concluded that the results were new and original, and presented them, in Maxwell's name, at the April meeting of the Royal Society of Edinburgh. (It was, one gathers, improper for a boy to lecture the Society in person.) After reading the paper, Forbes added the comment that Maxwell's method of constructing these curves was simpler than the scheme used by Descartes, and that these were the same ovals whose optical properties had been discussed by Newton and Huygens. All of which has made J. G. Crowther exclaim, in an essay on Maxwell: 'Descartes, Newton, Huygens! What names to appear in the discussion of a schoolboy's discovery!' Indeed.

This work was published under the title 'Oval Curves' in the April 1846 issue of the Royal Society of Edinburgh. The value of this paper is largely historical; it shows us in embryo the general character of Maxwell's talents. It teaches us too that his creative drive was stirring early. But it was clearly not a mathematically profound work; it was not beyond the technical abilities of a bright sixth-former. Maxwell was not a child prodigy like Gauss, Pascal or Mozart. His genius would mature more slowly.

At this point of his development, in the autumn of 1846, it might have been wise to take James out of the Academy; he was ready for university work. But his father, a cautious and conservative soul, must have felt that the benefits of a traditional education outweighed the uncertain advantages of university-level science and mathematics. He recognized his son's brilliance yet, most likely, he still wished James to follow in his own footsteps and go into law. Except at a few universities, the sciences did not then provide recognizable careers for bright young men; such posts as were available were poorly remunerated. One sympathizes with the dilemma faced by a doting father with so gifted an adolescent on his hands. We have the wisdom of hindsight.

The Royal Society reading by Forbes of James' paper was the start of an enduring friendship. Forbes was to take young Maxwell under his wing, guide his interests, help him in decisions, introduce him to people. Professionally speaking, this was the most important outside aid given Maxwell by anyone. Maxwell's talents were so great he would have succeeded on his own, without help; Forbes, however, smoothed the way. And while their paths eventually diverged – Forbes ended up as Principal of United College at St Andrews – Maxwell never forgot the older man's kindness. 'I loved that man' he confided to Lewis Campbell many years later, after Forbes' death.

At the age of fourteen, then, while still at school, Maxwell became involved in original, creative mathematical and scientific work. He spent a great deal of time on these activities, writing up some of his investigations in manuscript form, passing them on to Forbes or friends like P. G. Tait (the only one of his schoolfellows to understand these matters), making mechanical models, and reading a great deal. Years later Tait recorded his memories of Maxwell during these years:

> At school he was first regarded as shy and rather dull. He made no friendships, and he spent his occasional holidays in reading old ballads, drawing curious diagrams and making rude mechanical models. This absorbtion in such pursuits, totally unintelligible to his schoolfellows (who were quite innocent of mathematics) of course procured him a not very complimentary nickname, which I know is still remembered . . . About the middle of his school career, however, he surprised his companions by suddenly becoming the most brilliant among them . . . I still possess some of the manuscripts we exchanged in 1846 and early in 1847. Those by Maxwell are on 'The Conical Pendulum', 'Descartes' Ovals', 'Meloid and Apioid' and 'Trifocal Curves'. The three latter are connected with his first published paper, communicated by Forbes to this Society and printed in our Proceedings.

Creative activity inevitably interferes with the humdrum requirements of day-to-day life and Maxwell's school performance suffered; at least in 1846 he missed the Mathematical Medal. Nevertheless, he remained an outstanding student; when he left the Academy in 1847 he was first in Maths and English and very near the top in Latin. This was characteristic of Maxwell: he did what had to be done, and did it well. At the same time, he had a finely developed sense of priorities. For a boy of his gifts it would not have been difficult, and could have been tempting, to outshine his fellow students in all fields; but to do this he would have had to spend more time on swotting – muggery, he called it – and sacrifice at least some of his commitments to deeper interests, such as science or philosophy. And this he would not do. In early youth, as in the rest of his life, he maintained a steadfast, personal set of priorities that brooked no interference.

In those adolescent years Maxwell's intellectual life was one of great ferment. He read up on many fields: geology, mathematics, optics, Dryden, Swift and Hobbes. This early interest in philosophy reminds one again of Einstein – who, it is said, read and assimilated Kant's *Critique of Pure Reason* at the age of thirteen. Young James was in addition something of an athlete; he was a proficient horseman, and liked swimming and pole-vaulting. Lewis Campbell, who spent part of the 1846 summer holiday at Glenlair, was much impressed by his friend's virtuosity with the 'Devil on two sticks' (a device consisting of a string tied to two sticks, and used to throw, spin and catch a double cone of wood – a craze which at the end of the century became world-wide under the name of Diabolo). Other pastimes of James' at Glenlair were walking, driving his pony Meg around the countryside, teaching tricks to his dog Toby, and incessant talk. Reticent as he was with strangers, he was open and voluble with friends, discoursing on everything, from science and literature to metaphysics and religion.

From earliest childhood, Maxwell's private life was imbued with religion. Both his mother (an Episcopalian) and father (a Presbyterian) were devout churchgoers. Grace was said at mealtimes, and the master of the house read evening prayers to the assembled household. Church on Sundays was *de rigueur*; when in Glenlair, the family worshipped in the neighbouring village kirks of Corsock and Parton. Neither in his adolescence, nor in his later years, did Maxwell question the basic tenets of his Christian religion. The eventual combining, in one mind, of a unique level of scientific insight and sophistication with a simple, apparently unquestioning faith struck many as curious. Unfortunately most of one's information on Maxwell's religious convictions comes from Campbell, himself a minister, who stated firmly that in some domains he would not describe his friend's innermost feelings: these were things 'wherewith the stranger intermeddles not'. The deliberate omission of information is, of course, simply a way of cooking the facts – a cardinal sin for any biographer; one cannot help wishing, with J. G. Crowther, that Campbell could 'himself have avoided intermeddling with the biographical data of a world genius'. Maxwell's letters, though, suggest that his religious views were quite conventional; he always remained a devout churchgoer.

Scientists who have since attempted short biographies or essays on Maxwell have largely omitted the subject of his religion – passing it over, one assumes, in embarrassed silence. One should remember, however, that the other two greatest mathematical physicists of our culture – Newton and Einstein – were also moved by a religious or at least a mystical spirit. To think deeply about the universe leads inevitably to an awareness of great mysteries, of the mind's inability to cope with first questions. This does not necessarily bring one to accept some particular religious gospel. Einstein's faith, for instance, was unconventional; while he was a mystic, he rejected the conventional trappings of religion; but he believed in a God of sorts. Maxwell's religion, on the other hand, always remained traditional. Without wishing to psychologize the subject out of existence, there is much to be said for the security offered by serious faith. A seemingly meaningless universe is not a comforting concept; it would have been very hard to cope with for an introspective, sensitive and lonely adolescent like James Clerk Maxwell.

The historical background of Maxwell's childhood and youth was one of accelerating change. But in financial terms the Clerk Maxwells were well insulated. Political events played only a peripheral role in the life of James' family. Glenlair was the focus of their lives. As landowners they were comfortably off; theirs was mostly a rural existence – calm, gracious and genteel. To be sure, the industrial revolution was in full swing; inventions and new technology were sprouting everywhere – and this, with the running of the estate, supplied Maxwell's father with most of his active interest in the outside world. In Maxwell's life, or in that of his parents and close relatives, no clouds of financial worry darkened the horizon. It made little difference to them whether Russell was prime minister, or Peel, or Palmerston. The reinstitution of an income tax and tariff reforms by Peel (in 1842 and again in 1845), and the repeal of the corn laws in 1846 may have worried the Clerk Maxwells. No doubt they became slightly poorer for these events, but not significantly so. The split in the Church of Scotland and formation of the Free Church in 1843 were, in all probability, subjects of greater interest to them – more so than taxes, the vexing problems of Ireland, or the Chartists.

Scientific influences and developments – especially those taking place at the turn of the century and during his adolescence – were far more important in determining the course of Maxwell's life and career. From the age of fourteen onwards, through his regular attendance at Royal Society meetings, Maxwell absorbed a steady stream of scientific information. Occasionally a special event, some particularly stimulating lecture, exposed him to the forefront of contemporary research. One such was a talk in March 1847 on the Adams–Le Verrier discovery of Neptune – an interesting story for at least two reasons. As a demonstration of the power of mathematical analysis applied to nature it was striking – *sublime*, was the word used by Sir George Airy, the astronomer royal. At the same time, it was a stark warning of how easily narrow, petty issues, personal or national vanities could mar a beautiful accomplishment. The affair may be summarized as follows.

Irregularities in the motion of the planet Uranus had been noted soon after its discovery by William Herschel (1781). No matter how carefully one calculated the perturbations due to known planets, its orbit showed substantial and systematic departures from the predictions of Newtonian mechanics. These apparent inconsistencies in an otherwise splendidly accurate theory were worrisome; either, in the far reaches of the solar system Newton's laws were invalid, or there was another planet circling the sun beyond Uranus' orbit. The chief difficulty lay in the great complexity of the calculations needed to test this last hypothesis. A young Cambridge don, John Couch Adams, was the first to carry these out successfully; with the use of plausible assumptions, he succeeded in predicting to within a couple of degrees the correct position of the undiscovered planet for 1 October 1845. It was a brilliant job, but for a variety of reasons Adams failed to persuade Sir George Airy or others to institute the search; had they bothered to peer through their telescopes, they would have found the planet where Adams had said it would be. In the meantime, Leverrier in France had carried out similar calculations and had persuaded the Berlin observatory to look for it. The search was immediately successful and the discovery was announced by Leverrier on 1 October 1846. Airy pointed out that Adams had, in fact, predicted the correct position of the planet a whole year earlier. The French paper *Le National* then accused British astronomers of organizing a miserable plot to steal the discovery from Leverrier. Arago, one of France's foremost scientists, proposed to name the planet after the French astronomer. The whole thing became a grandiose squabble, which has been described by a more recent astronomer royal, Sir Harold Spencer Jones, as 'A comedy of confusion, fecklessness, donnish hairpulling, Gallic backbiting, stuffiness, jealousy and general academic blight' – an unsublime conclusion to a sublime piece of work. The only participant to come out of it with credit was Adams himself, who stayed quietly aloof throughout the fracas. An academic honour was bestowed upon him some years later: a competitive Cambridge prize was named for him – the Adams Prize 'for the best essay on some subject of pure mathematics, astronomy or other branch of natural philosophy'.

Maxwell, aged fifteen at the time of the lecture, was much impressed by this scientific accomplishment – a remarkable vindication of Newtonian theory and a convincing display of the power of mathematical analysis. In ten years time he would make an equally elegant and impressive contribution to celestial mechanics with his work on Saturn's rings – and would for this be one of the first recipients of the Adams Prize.

The first decades of Maxwell's century were rich in new and fundamental scientific developments. By modern standards the total volume of work being published was still small: an able, well-informed person could keep abreast of major advances. But the pace was quickening; discoveries followed each other in quick succession; many of these were to be of direct relevance to Maxwell's future work.

During his last year at the Academy, Maxwell became actively interested in optics – an echo, one assumes, of his early childhood fascination with light. His interest, at this stage, was intensely practical, consisting of experiments carried out at Old 31 and in his attic laboratory at Glenlair. The colours of the spectrum, obtained by the dispersion of light in prisms, intrigued him greatly; his life-long preoccupation with colour appears to date from this period. For a while he, too, was much taken with Newton's rings – multicoloured, circular patterns seen in white light through a plano-convex lens pressed onto a glass surface, which could be neatly explained by the wave theory of light. Optics had received great impetus, not long before Maxwell's birth, thanks to the work of Fresnel in France, Young in England, and Fraunhofer in Germany: the wave theory of light was well established by the time of his youth.

Even though the precise nature of these waves would remain a mystery until Maxwell's own work of the 1860s, there was little doubt that light consisted of some kind of travelling vibrations. It had not proved possible to describe a physical medium, a *substance* with the necessary properties to support such waves; nevertheless it was already understood that these vibrations had to be, in some sense, transverse to the direction of travel of the wave. Crystals, it had been shown, could change the orientation of these vibrations, i.e. they could alter the *polarization* of the light wave. Iceland spar, for instance, takes the light falling on it and splits it into two differently refracted parts, having different polarization. Maxwell's interest in this was considerable: here was a phenomenon which proved the transverse nature of light without, however, explaining how or why these vibrations took place. To one of his physical intuition, this was a peculiarly intriguing effect, pointing to hidden depths in the theory of light. Yet, though not fully understood, polarization was already exploited in practice. James Nicol of Edinburgh had invented a method for polarizing light in a desired direction by cutting prisms of Iceland spar in special ways. These prisms, a boon to generations of mineralogists and geologists (who use polarized light for identifying minerals under the microscope), would become known as nicols. An uncle, John Cay, introduced young Maxwell in 1846 to Nicol – who was so impressed by the boy that he made him a gift of a pair of his polarizing prisms; Maxwell treasured them for the rest of his life.

A great deal of revolutionary work was afoot in science during these years of Maxwell's boyhood. Faraday, for instance, was still completing his experimental researches on electromagnetism. His long drawn-out, painstaking investigations following the discovery of magnetic induction led to a beautiful, lucid description of the observed properties of electricity and magnetism. In a few years Maxwell would become acquainted with Faraday's results – the foundation of his own future masterpiece: the theory of the electromagnetic field and the greatest of the great nineteenth-century syntheses. In the meantime other, almost equally far-reaching, advances were taking place in mechanics, the physics of heat, and the theory of gases, to all of which Maxwell would also contribute. The concepts of thermodynamics and the philosophically profound principle of conservation of energy date from this era; without these, modern science would not exist.

As the name implies, thermodynamics deals with the motion and properties of heat. Yet heat is energy, and as the discipline developed it was seen that its scope and relevance were far greater: it was to be not merely the science of heat, but of energy itself. With electromagnetism and mechanics, it became a cornerstone of man's thinking about the universe.

The birth of thermodynamics was spurred at the end of the eighteenth century by James Watt's invention of the steam engine – a good example of technology leading and illuminating science. Sadi Carnot in France thought deeply about steam engines and in 1824 published a treatise entitled *Réflexions sur la Puissance Motrice du Feu* – literally *The Motive Power of Fire* – which laid the groundwork for thermodynamics. He examined the *efficiency* of steam engines; he showed that work could be done only by transferring heat between different temperatures. He also saw that heat was a form of energy. Unfortunately he died of cholera in 1832 at the age of thirty-six, not having had time to publish his determination of the mechanical equivalent of heat – which is the precise translation of calories into units of mechanical energy. The credit for this was to be shared by several contemporaries of Maxwell: Robert Mayer, a German ship's doctor, Robert Prescott Joule, an exceptionally gifted British scientist of independent means, and von Helmholtz – a German physiologist and physicist. Working in the 1840s, all three offered proof and measurements of this equivalence. Joule's work was perhaps the most thorough; he offered simple, solid experimental proof of the equivalence of heat and energy, made careful measurements and thereby demonstrated that, in an isolated system, the total energy stays constant. This was the *conservation of energy*, one of the most far-reaching and powerful principles of modern science, and the basis of the first law of thermodynamics. It has offered guidance to all of our science and technology; it has also profoundly influenced the industrial and economic world.

Carnot had emphasized, too, that what matters in practical terms is the availability of energy – which, it turned out, could be measured with the help of a new concept, introduced by Clausius in 1850: the *entropy*. This is a direct measure of the unavailability of energy: the greater the entropy of a system, the less available is its energy. Later Boltzmann, another great nineteenth century German physicist, would show that in many cases entropy is also a measure of disorder. The connection between disorder, entropy and energy availability is easily grasped if you think of a collection of engine parts strewn over a garage floor: disorder is high, entropy is large, you do not have a working engine, the availability of energy is low. Put the parts together in the proper order: you now have an ordered system, entropy is low, the engine will run, energy is easily available. In the same way, if you take a crystal and grind it to powder, you increase its entropy; the rusted hulk of a steam engine in the junkyard has more entropy than when it was new. Of particular concern to all who like to contemplate the broad issues of life and death, the future of the universe and philosophical questions of this kind, is the *second law of thermodynamics* which says that the entropy of isolated systems must always increase: decay and disorder rule the universe. Eventually, the suns and their planets, the nebulae and the galaxies, must all return to chaos. The cosmos must ineluctably run down – or so it seems, if we take the second law at face value: disordered systems are simply more likely than ordered ones. Yet there may be, within a complex system, localized nuclei in which, for a while, order may prevail; crystals form small, temporary havens within this realm of universal disintegration. And such, of course, is life: a short-lived, temporary repeal of the second law of thermodynamics, until ashes go back to ashes and dust to dust.

Thermodynamics is, for a physicist, an edifice of singular beauty – the prototype of the perfect deductive theory, which builds a powerful, general, and rigorous body of science, whilst starting from a few simple laws. In this it resembles Euclidean geometry, but is more sophisticated and subtle; geometry, after all, deals only with the static properties of space; thermodynamics attends to matter in space and time, and touches upon some of the most profound cosmic issues. One or two of these, like the second law and the ultimate running-down of the universe, would one day greatly intrigue Maxwell.

Some of science's deepest insights were developed, then, during Maxwell's youth and early adulthood: the conservation of energy, the second law of thermodynamics, Darwin's principle of evolution through natural selection. Yet the scientists of Maxwell's era were not, on the whole, philosophically inclined; these were practical times, times of intense technological optimism. Knowledge was power, and technical muscle was powering the industrial age. Nineteenth century physicists were mostly determinedly empiricist, largely innocent of philosophy and hostile to metaphysics. In this, as in his religious views, Maxwell differed from most of his colleagues. Not only was he reading Hobbes at the age of fourteen – he also remained throughout his life deeply concerned with the philosophical issues raised by science. These leanings doubtless had much to do with the profundity and originality of his later, mature work. Their development was greatly encouraged by his university years in Edinburgh.

4

MATURING TALENT

Dear old Academy,
Queer old Academy,
A merry lot we were, I wot,
When at the old Academy

. . .

Let pedants seek for scraps of Greek,
    Their lingo to Macademize;
Gie me the sense, without pretence,
    That comes o' Scots Academies.

Let scholars all, both grit and small,
    Of learning mourn the sad demise;
That's as they think, but we will drink
    Good luck to Scots Academies.

Thus at the age of sixteen young Maxwell celebrated his departure from the Edinburgh Academy – with a poem. It has an ironic edge, though this is not directed against the school. It actually displays a certain generosity. A lesser spirit could have harboured resentment at the treatment he had received in his early years at the Academy. Maxwell was a forgiving soul and, in the flush of pleasure at this move to greener pastures, the past did not rankle. But during and after the July prizegiving he appears to have been quite ill. His father described the disorder as a 'fever fit' and assumed it was due to nervous exhaustion following the exams. Maxwell's health was never strong and the effects of intellectual strain were to plague him for many years. A summer at Glenlair quickly restored his health.

In October 1847 Maxwell returned to 31 Heriot Row and became a student at the University of Edinburgh. Founded by royal charter in the late sixteenth century, this is the youngest of the old Scottish universities – a scatter of grey buildings in the centre of town, with a handsome central quadrangle enclosed in an early Georgian magnificence of arches, friezes and Grecian colonnades. Here James took courses in logic and metaphysics from Sir William Hamilton, natural philosophy (physics) from Forbes and mathematics from Kelland. Sir William Hamilton (1788–1856) the Scottish philosopher and metaphysician is not to be confused with an archaeologist of the same name or with the great Irish mathematician Sir William Rowan Hamilton (1805–65).

Forbes knew well the boy's intelligence and originality – which was perceived also by relatives, friends and fellow-students like P. G. Tait and Robert Campbell (Lewis' brother). They all understood, in the words of one, that Maxwell was fated to be 'a discoverer in Natural Philosophy and a very original worker in Mathematics'. Forbes, a constant source of encouragement, helped broaden the boy's knowledge of experimental physics. Maxwell developed a special rapport with him, staying long after hours and using university apparatus for experiments.

Forbes and Hamilton were the formative influences on Maxwell's early development as a scientist. It is interesting that these two men, who disliked each other intensely, stood for quite different views on education and philosophy – views which were then battling for supremacy in Scottish higher education, especially in mathematics and the sciences. Hamilton was of the venerable Scottish tradition which stressed the importance of insight into the philosophical foundations of mathematics and gave less importance to mere technical skill or manipulative expertise. This attitude was part of an overall approach to higher education which emphasized examination of fundamentals in all subjects and encouraged freewheeling discussions between the professors and their classes – a system viewed with disapproval by the English, who thought it conducive to inadequate expertise, superficiality and perhaps even anarchic tendencies. A Scotsman too, Forbes had been to Cambridge and was a protégé of William Whewell, Master of Trinity, influential historian of science and philosopher, and a man who held strong views on the laxity of Scottish higher education. Forbes had won a close-fought academic battle with Hamilton over the recently vacated chair of mathematics. He succeeded in getting the post for his own candidate – Kelland, also a Cambridge man who, though a competent teacher, was not a first-rate mathematician. (He owed much of his reputation to an attack on Fourier's work – an attack which the young W. Thomson had shown to have been seriously in error.)

Forbes represented the modern respect for technique – without which science and technology cannot advance. Hamilton, on the other hand, stood for the need to understand the foundations of knowledge – the ground upon which science stands; and in Maxwell he found an answering chord. Hamilton's lectures stimulated Maxwell's philosophical bent and set him thinking carefully about the nature of science, giving him a sort of basic epistemological concern rare among scientists of his time – or ours, for that matter. Thus in April 1850 he outlines to Campbell the programme of study he will pursue during the spring and summer. This includes, under the heading of *Metaphysics*:

> Kant's *Kritik of Pure Reason* in German, read with a determination to make it agree with Sir W. Hamilton.

In another letter, written a few months later – shortly before his nineteenth birthday, he shows a well-matured interest in these matters and adumbrates some future insights:

I was thinking today of the duties of the cognitive faculty. It is universally admitted that duties are voluntary, and that the will governs understanding by giving or withholding Attention. They say that Understanding ought to work by the rules of right reason. These rules are, or ought to be, contained in Logic; but the actual science of Logic is conversant at present only with things either certain, impossible or *entirely* doubtful, none of which (fortunately) we have to reason on. Therefore the true logic of this world is the Calculus of Probabilities, which takes account of the magnitude of the probability (which is, or which ought to be in a reasonable man's mind). This branch of Math., which is generally thought to favour gambling, dicing, and wagering, and therefore highly immoral, is the only 'Mathematics for Practical Men', as we ought to be. Now, as human knowledge comes by the senses in such a way that the existence of things external is only inferred from the harmonious (not similar) testimony of the different senses, Understanding, acting by the laws of right reason, will assign to different truths (or facts, or testimonies, or what shall I call them) different degrees of probability. Now, as the senses give new testimonies continually, and as no man ever detected in them any real inconsistency, it follows that the probability and *credibility* of their testimony is increasing day by day, and the more a man uses them the more he believes them. He believes them. What is believing? When the probability (there is no better word found) in a man's mind of a certain proposition being true is greater than that of its being false, he believes it with a proportion of faith corresponding to the probability, and this probability may be increased or diminished by new facts. This is faith in general. When a man thinks he has enough evidence for some notion of his he sometimes refuses to listen to any additional evidence *pro* or *con*, saying, 'It is a settled question, *probatis probata*; it needs no evidence; it is certain.' This is knowledge as distinguished from faith. He says, 'I do not believe; I know.' 'If any man thinketh that he knoweth, he knoweth yet nothing as he ought to know.' This knowledge is a shutting of one's ears to all arguments, and is the same as 'Implicit faith' in one of its meanings. 'Childlike faith,' confounded with it, is not credulity, for children are not credulous, but find out sooner than some think that many men are liars.

A historian could point out here that in the nineteenth century science was regarded as justificationist – i.e. scientists tended to believe that the use of inductive logic could, starting from 'hard facts', *prove* a scientific theory – a view no longer popular among philosophers of science. At the age of eighteen Maxwell was already dubious of this approach: we see him proposing an alternative (now called probabilism), which says that, while theories are unprovable, each has a certain probability of being true. This is an improvement on naive justificationism; but it too is no longer held in much esteem by epistemologists. Yet to call Maxwell a probabilist (or, as some would say, a neo-justificationist) would be an oversimplification. Indeed the apposite and startling introduction of a biblical quote shows that he was actually sceptical of science's ability to lead to *certainty* in knowledge. In this he foreshadows modern scientific philosophers. Nevertheless, it is difficult to categorize Maxwell's philosophy of science; and the more one learns of him, the harder it becomes.

Earlier than the above is an essay, submitted to Hamilton, entitled 'On the Properties of Matter'. Of special interest are young Maxwell's (he was then seventeen) comments on *force*:

> Of forces acting between two particles of matter there are several kinds.
> The first kind is independent of the quality of the particles, and depends solely on their masses and mutual distance. Of this kind is the attraction of gravitation . . .
> The second kind depends on the quality of the particles; of this kind are the attractions of magnetism, electricity and chemical affinity, which are all convertible into one another and affect all bodies.
> The third kind acts between particles of the same body, and tends to keep them at a certain distance from one another and in a certain configuration.

Forces of the third kind, we now know, are a particular case of the second; but the electromagnetic nature of atoms and molecules was not well understood at the time, and this represents an accurate statement of contemporary views on matter. Particularly interesting is Maxwell's grasp of the basic difference between the forces of gravitation and electricity and magnetism, and of the convertibility of magnetic and electric forces into one another, as well as their relationship to chemical affinity. It seems probable from this, as well as from independent statements made by Campbell, that Maxwell's first acquaintance with Faraday's work dates from these years.

At Edinburgh, then, Maxwell learned logic, physics, metaphysics, a quantity of maths and chemistry, and some geology. If one adds to this a prior and thorough grounding in Greek and Latin, omnivorous and extensive reading, his erudition by the age of eighteen was by our standards astonishing. By this time too it was obvious that his chief enthusiasm was for science. He spent much time building apparatus and worrying about basic theory and mathematical problems (or propositions – *props*, he called them). During holidays he ran a variety of experiments in his garret at Glenlair, which he described in a letter to Lewis Campbell:

> I have regularly set up shop now above the wash-house at the gate, in a garret. I have an old door set on two barrels, and two chairs, of which one is safe, and a skylight above, which will slide up and down.
>
> On the door (or table) there is a lot of bowls, jugs, plates, jam pigs [jars] etc., containing water, salt, soda, sulphuric acid, blue vitriol, plumbago ore; also broken glass, iron, and copper wire, copper and zinc plate, bees' wax, sealing wax, clay, rosin, charcoal, a lens, a Smee's Galvanic apparatus, and a countless variety of little beetles, spiders, and wood lice, which fall into the different liquids and poison themselves. I intend to get up some more galvanism in jam pigs; but I must first copper the interior of the pigs, so am experimenting on the best methods of electrotyping. So I am making copper seals with the device of a beetle. First, I thought a beetle was a good conductor, so I embedded one in wax (not at all cruel, because I slew him in boiling water in which he never kicked), leaving his back out; but he would not do. Then I took a cast of him in sealing wax, and pressed the wax into the hollow, and black-leaded it with a brush; but neither would that do. So at last I took my fingers and rubbed it, which I find the best way to use the black lead. Then it coppered famously. I melt out the wax with a lens, that being the cleanest way of getting a strong heat, so I do most things with it that need heat. To-day I astonished the natives as follows. I took a crystal of blue vitriol and put the lens to it, and so drove off the water, leaving a white powder. Then I did the same to some washing soda, and mixed the two white powders together; and made a small native spit on them,

which turned them green by a mutual exchange, thus: – 1. Sulphate of copper and carbonate of soda. 2. Sulphate of soda and carbonate of copper (blue or green).

With regard to electro-magnetism you may tell Bob that I have not begun the machine he speaks of, being occupied with better plans, one of which is rather down cast, however, because the machine when tried went a bit and stuck; and I did not find the impediment till I had dreamt over it properly, which I consider the best mode of resolving difficulties of a particular kind, which may be found out by thought, or especially by the laws of association. Thus you are going along the road with a key in your pocket. You hear a clink behind you, but do not look around, thinking it nothing in particular; when you get home the key is gone; so you dream it all over, and though you have forgotten everything else, you remember the look of the place, but do not remember the locality (that is, as thus, 'Near a large thistle on the left side of the road' – nowhere in particular, but so that it can be found). Next day comes a woman from the peats who has found the key in a corresponding place. This is not 'believing in dreams', for the dream did not point out the place by the general locality, but by the lie of the ground.

Please to write and tell how Academy matters go, if they are coming to a head. I am reading Herodotus, Euterpe, having taken the turn; that is to say, that sometimes I can do props, read diff. and Int. Calc., Poisson, Hamilton's dissertations, etc. Off, then I take back to experiments, history of what you may call it, make up leeway in the newspapers, read Herodotus, and draw figures of the curves above. Oh deary, 11 P.M.! Hoping to see you *before* October . . . I defer till tomorrow.

July 6. To-day I have set on to the coppering of the jam pig which I polished yesterday.

I have stuck in the wires better than ever, and it is going on at a great rate, being a rainy day, and the skylight shut and a smell of hydrogen gas. I have left it for an hour to read Poisson, as I am pleased with him today. Sometimes I do not like him, because he pretends to give information as to calculations of sorts, whereas he only tells how it might be done if you were allowed an infinite time to do it in, as well as patience. Of course he never stoops to give a particular example or even class of them. He tells lies about the way people make barometers, etc.

While Maxwell's world was busily expanding and his view of science maturing, his creativity was also blooming. Another geometrical paper, on *Rolling Curves*, was presented for him to the Royal Society of Edinburgh by Kelland. Like its predecessor this was principally a clever exercise in geometry; its interest is chiefly historical. His next effort on *The Equilibrium of Elastic Solids* which he wrote in 1849–50, is a more interesting piece of work; it was, indeed, the kind of paper any good nineteenth century scientist would have been pleased with. It is not in a class with his later work, but it shows already considerable talent. The thoroughness and physical insight it displays, in particular, are impressive. The mathematics show understanding, if not yet originality or real craftsmanship: they are largely applications of previous results by G. G. Stokes.

Stokes – a household name amongst theoretical physicists and an important figure of nineteenth century science – had, a few years before Maxwell's paper, established the correct equations describing the deformation of solids subjected to stress. These relations – a physicist would call them the field equations of elasticity – are in some ways analogous to those of the electromagnetic field; a fact which of course could not be appreciated at the time. It is intriguing, however, that Maxwell became involved in their study at this early, formative stage of his career. He was, most likely unconsciously, cutting his teeth on the theory of elasticity, developing insight into the properties of fields and acquiring the mathematical tools he was going to need in years to come.

The current system by which journal editors, to gauge the suitability of an article, submit it to a referee, was already in use; Forbes, as editor of the *Transactions* of the Royal Society of Edinburgh, sent Maxwell's manuscript to Kelland. After the latter had returned it, this is what Forbes wrote to Maxwell:

> Edinburgh, 4th May 1850
> My Dear Sir, Professor Kelland, to whom your paper was referred by the Council R.S., reports favourably upon it, but complains of the great obscurity of several parts, owing to the *abrupt transitions* and want of distinction between what is *assumed* and what is *proven* in various passages, which he has marked in pencil, and which I trust you will use your utmost effort to make plain and intelligible. It is perfectly evident that it must be useless to publish a paper for the use of scientific readers

generally, the steps of which cannot, in many places, be followed by so expert an algebraist as Prof. Kelland; – if, indeed, they be *steps* at all and not assumptions of theorems from other writers who are not quoted. You will please pay particular attention to clear up these passages, and return the MS by post to Professor Kelland, West Cottage, Wardie, Edinburgh, so that he may receive it by Saturday the 11th, as I shall then have left town.   Believe me, yours sincerely,

James D. Forbes

The tone is formal, in places acidulous – Forbes was treating his protégé as he would any author. Obviously the referee had a hard time with parts of the manuscript. Whether the trouble lay in Maxwell's original exposition or in Kelland's private intellectual difficulties is not clear – a common enough and unresolvable problem of the refereeing system. But by our current standards of scientific writing – which admittedly are not high – Maxwell's published version is actually a model of clarity. In it he applied Stokes' equations to a number of typical problems, the answers to which he verified experimentally. This he did with a series of transparent stressed plates, using polarized light – obtaining splendid irridescent patterns, some of which he recorded in watercolour. This, one of the earliest applications of photoelasticity, had a curious by-product: Maxwell copied one of these patterns as a colourful design of woolwork for a kettle-holder, which hung for a while by his fireplace in Glenlair.

At the university young Maxwell was under no pressure. His studies left him time and freedom to pursue other interests, to explore and develop his scientific abilities in directions of his choice – along lines which would one day help him in his greatest work: the theory of electromagnetism, with its re-markable insights into the properties of fields and the nature of light.

As an Edinburgh University student, already Maxwell's knowledge and understanding were impressive: yet these needed organizing and disciplining. It has been suggested that, in this respect, the instruction he received was deficient – not thorough or systematic enough. During these years, Maxwell acquired considerable mathematical equipment; he seems to have done much of this on his own, reading the works of contemporary mathematical physicists like W. R. Hamilton, Poisson or Fourier. He *could* have used an experienced hand to guide and exercise his talents. The opinion of his Cambridge coach would be that, after three years at Edinburgh, he still lacked the real craftsman's command of his tools. For great science, truly creative science, is far more like art than is commonly thought. It is a combination of technique and inspiration, of high craft and creativity. To be an outstanding musician, one must start young and do one's scales and practice – practice constantly, every day of one's life. To be a great mathematical physicist one must likewise master one's instrument, which is mathematics; without technique, inspiration is stillborn. The comparative importance of inspiration and technical mastery can be, and is, debated *ad infinitum*. It is frequently pointed out that both Einstein and Maxwell were stronger on physical intuition than in mathematics. Einstein had to acquire some of his tools – like tensor theory – as he pursued his physical insights and Maxwell, it is said, made many a mathematical slip in his manuscripts. This is so. Yet these are relative concepts; compared to most scientists, both had a better than average mathematical competence: without this they would have been powerless to express their inspiration. No one has solved the problem of creativity, of how to teach, foster or encourage it. Skill and competence, however, can be taught. Today, more than a century after Maxwell's death, a number of our universities can and do turn out technically competent, if not necessarily inspired, applied mathematicians and theoretical physicists. But in Maxwell's time, only one British university had a tradition of producing technical mastery in mathematics: this was Cambridge.

Nevertheless, Mr Clerk Maxwell was for several years reluctant to send his son to an unfamiliar, distant institution. He was a pious man and feared the influences to which James might be subjected. The controversial doctrines of Pusey, the

Oxford divine, were spreading throughout the Anglican church. Impiety he feared was rampant in scientific and university circles. Besides, James' furture career had not been decided upon – it still seemed possible that he would be a Scottish lawyer. And studying in Edinburgh was convenient. James, after all, was housed *en famille*, within travelling distance of Glenlair, within reach of parental influence and support. Mr Clerk Maxwell had always had a predilection for the path of least resistance and, as he grew older, the tendency had grown stronger. As Campbell put it, 'the habit of *inertia* had grown upon him'. Still, his worries over his son were sincere. At eighteen James was an odd young man:

> James Clerk Maxwell still occasioned some concern to the more conventional amongst his friends by the originality and simplicity of his ways. His replies in ordinary conversation were indirect and enigmatical, often uttered with hesitation and in a monotonous key. While extremely neat in person, he had a rooted objection to the vanities of starch and gloves. He had a pious horror of destroying anything – even a scrap of writing paper. He preferred travelling by the third class in railway journeys, saying he liked a hard seat. When at table he often seemed abstracted from what was going on, being absorbed in observing the effects of refracted light in the finger-glasses, or in trying some experiment with his eyes – seeing around a corner, making invisible stereoscopes, and the like. Miss Cay used to call his attention by crying, 'Jamsie, you're in a prop' He never tasted wine; and he spoke to gentle and simple in exactly the same tone.

Mrs Morrieson (Campbell's Mother) made in her diary the following reflection prior to Maxwell's departure to Cambridge:

> His manners are very peculiar; but having good sense, sterling worth, and good humour, the intercourse with a College world will rub off his oddities. I doubt not of his becoming a distinguished man.

Behind the eccentric exterior, the quirks and the precocious erudition, there lurked a fine, captivating sense of humour – a love of fun which surfaces irrepressibly in letters, poems and puns. The puns, to which he was addicted in youth, were mostly spoken and are lost to us. The poems preserve, here and there, a few lines of gentle humour. And there are nice touches in his letters, as when he complains to Campbell of his pen:

> It is possible that you may get a more full account of all these things (if agreeable) when I fall in with a pen that will spell; my present instrument partakes of the nature of skates, and I can hardly steer it.

And when he reports on his father's indecision with respect to Cambridge:

> the Cambridge scheme has been howked up from its repose in the regions of abortions, and is as far forward as an inspection of the Cambridge *Calendar* and a communication with Cantabs.

By the winter of 1850, though, many people, including Maxwell himself, were prodding his father to send him on to Cambridge. Forbes, in particular, paid a special visit to Mr Clerk Maxwell to persuade him. And so, after consultations with Professors Kelland, Blackburn, W. Thomson (who was at the University of Glasgow), not to mention a future bishop of Natal, the decision was made. In October 1850 Maxwell departed for Cambridge.

5

CAMBRIDGE

The bustle of modern commerce has encroached on Cambridge. Cars thread their way through the narrow streets, and every available nook is filled with parked vehicles. Yet, in comparison with much of our civilization, the university itself remains peaceful, stunningly handsome, a town unto itself, soaked in history and tradition, boasting sixteen colleges predating Newton – a collection of architectural jewels, chapels, gothic spires, medieval arches, ancient pavements hollowed and worn smooth by countless generations of busy dons and students, carefully tended lawns and, flowing through it all, the gentle Cam. And if parts of Cambridge are beautiful still, how much more so they must have been in Maxwell's day, before the modern annexes were squeezed in and motorized traffic invaded its streets! Whether, or in what manner, Maxwell was touched by this beauty, we don't know. Perhaps he was for a while homesick; but he quickly took to Cambridge and flourished there. And Cambridge, with its long tradition of tolerance for gifted eccentricity, took to him.

Well into our century, if you aspired to the best mathematical training offered in the English-speaking world, you went to Cambridge. Today this is no longer so; a handful of universities in North America and Britain do as well or better. But in Maxwell's youth, Cambridge was the best. When in the autumn of 1850 he arrived at Peterhouse – the university's oldest college, founded in 1284 – Cambridge had dominated British mathematics, and its ancillary disciplines like mechanics and astronomy, since Newton's time. As a training ground for mathematicians it was unexcelled – the standards were thorough, the grooming rigorous. In the eighteenth and early nineteenth centuries it had slipped a little – losing for a while some of its international pre-eminence; Newton's shadow had been a long one and, it has been said, had tended to stultify British originality. First-rate work continued to be done in Britain: mathematicians like Maclaurin, chemists like Dalton, physicists like Faraday and Joule were the equals of any. However in mathematics and mathematical physics (there was then no real distinction) the centre of gravity had shifted to the continent. Most of the progress was taking place in France (Lagrange, Laplace, Poisson, Cauchy, Fourier, Fresnel), Germany (Bessel, Gauss) or Switzerland (Euler, the Bernouillis). While not breaking with mechanistic Newtonian tradition, the Europeans had developed and applied a new spectrum of mathematical tools which by the 1820s were beginning to be used by physicists everywhere. Cambridge then awoke from its dogmatic Newtonian slumber and soon caught up. By the time Maxwell arrived at the university it again ranked high in international mathematics – particularly in applied mathematics, a discipline which then concerned itself chiefly with the problems of physics, mechanics and astronomy.

Among its particular strengths as an institution was the inculcation of mathematical techniques. Indeed, the problem-solving agility expected of a nineteenth-century undergraduate at the tripos examinations verged on virtuosity; today we tend to regard such extreme demands as unwise – discouraging to less quick and self-confident, yet potentially creative intellects. But Maxwell's mind was both profound and mathematically agile; Cambridge gave him exactly the kind of discipline he needed most.

Peterhouse was a small college with a high quota of mathematics students. Maxwell probably found the company there rather too specialized for his eclectic tastes. Since he wanted also to be sure of a fellowship some years hence, he moved to Trinity after a few months. The Master was William Whewell, a distinguished philosopher and scientist of broad interests and accomplishments (who, in the 1820s and 1830s had corresponded with Forbes and encouraged him to alter the emphasis in Scottish higher education). Training for the maths tripos was ferocious, as was the competition amongst tutors trying to produce the most top graduates or wranglers. Maxwell eventually became the fifteenth member of William Hopkins' 'team' of undergraduates. Hopkins belonged to that peculiarly English tradition of great Oxford and Cambridge tutors – an essential breed for the survival of first-rate higher education on British lines. A geophysicist and applied mathematician, he had a special talent for singling out and preparing the most promising students and had a long list of first wranglers to his credit. Hopkins' impressions of Maxwell, recorded in the reminiscences of a fellow-student, are thus particularly interesting:

> He [Hopkins] was talking to me this evening about Maxwell. He says he is unquestionably the most extraordinary man he has met within the whole range of his experience; he says it appears impossible for Maxwell to think incorrectly on physical subjects; that in his analysis [1], however, he is far more deficient; he looks upon him as a great genius, with all its eccentricities, and prophesies that one day he will shine as a light in physical science, a prophecy in which all his fellow-students strenuously unite. [(1) 'Analysis' was a term used well into the twentieth century for the branch of mathematics most useful in classical physics. Maxwell's technique, in other words, needed polishing.]

There is at Trinity a photograph of Maxwell as an undergraduate sitting on a chair, probably in the college court. He is holding a top – a tool he used to great advantage in his experiments on colour. The picture is taken from the side, and shows a fine straight-nosed profile. His gaze is focused on something out of the picture; the expression is a trifle distracted and distant – but this could be due to his shortsightedness. His complexion, it is reported, was sallow, his hair raven black and his eyes a deep brown. By the spring of 1852 he grew an incipient beard with, says Campbell, 'a crisp strength in each particular hair, that gave him more the look of a Nazarite than a nineteenth century youth'. But in this picture he is still beardless and his jaw is square and strong; a half-smile plays about the mouth, giving the whole a gently humorous, somewhat introverted expression. He was short – about five foot four – strong and athletic; an attractive, wholesome-looking young man.

When he arrived at the university in the autumn of 1850, he brought with him all his experimental bric-à-brac – what Jeans has referred to rather disdainfully as 'Maxwell's experimental litter' and his family called 'Jamsie's dirt'. Campbell describes it as 'scraps of gelatine, gutta-percha, and unannealed glass, his bits of magnetized steel and other objects' which appeared to many as 'matter in the wrong place'.

There is little doubt that Maxwell struck most of his Cambridge contemporaries as a queer fish. According to Professor Swan, who heard him talk at a meeting in Edinburgh in 1850: 'His utterance . . . would be somewhat spasmodic in character, as it continued to be in later times, his words coming in sudden gushes with notable pauses in between . . . ' His accent was Scots – so broad that his first reading of the lesson in chapel caused considerable untoward merriment amongst all, including the College Master.

Conscious of the need to keep his body active, Maxwell was an ardent swimmer. He used to bathe in the Cam – a fairly orthodox relaxation among undergraduates. However his diving methods were distinctive. Says P. G. Tait:

> He used to go up the pollard at the bathing shed, throw himself *flat on his face* in the water, dive and cross, then ascend on the pollard on the other side, project himself *flat on his back* in the water. He said it stimulated the circulation.

For some time, despite contrary advice from his father, he maintained at Trinity a routine of late study, exercising around 2.30 a.m. in the college itself. A contemporary reports that:

> From 2 to 2.30 a.m. he took exercise by running along the upper corridor, *down* the stairs, along the lower corridor, then *up* the stairs, and so on, until the inhabitants of the rooms along his track got up and lay *perdus* behind their sporting-doors to have shots at him with boots, hair-brushes, etc., as he passed.

It is not clear how long Maxwell kept to this particular practice. Certainly he continued then, and through most of his life, the habit of working late at night. Because of his odd hours he had at least one brush with the authorities, in the person of the senior dean, one J. A. Frere. This good man appears to have sent him a note, reprimanding him for skipping the occasional chapel. Maxwell atoned with a brief letter of apology, pointing out politely that these sins of omission had been due, in part, to his late hours of study. But the incident must have rankled for he produced in the following year a somewhat waspish poem celebrating the senior dean's move to Shillington, a poem written *à la manière de* Burns' *John Anderson*:

> John Alexander Frere, John,
>   When we were first acquent
> You lectured us as Freshmen
>   In the holy term of Lent;
> But now you're gettin' bald John,
>   Your end is drawing near,
> And I think we'd better say 'Goodbye,
>   John Alexander Frere.'

> .   .   .

> The Lecture Room no more, John,
>   Shall hear thy drowsy tone,
> No more shall men in Chapel
>   Bow before thy throne.

But Shillington with meekness,
    The oracle shall hear,
That set St Mary's all to sleep –
    John Alexander Frere.

Then once before we part, John,
    Let all be clean forgot,
Our scandalous inventions
    (Thy note-lets, prized or not).
For under all conventions,
    The small man lived sincere,
The kernel of the Senior Dean,
    John Alexander Frere.

When inspired, Maxwell had a fine way with words and a sharp tongue. But the image conveyed by his contemporaries is one of genuine friendliness and lack of pretension. The Revd H. M. Butler, who became headmaster of Harrow as well as Master of Trinity, would remember Maxwell in these terms:

His position among us . . . was unique. He was the one acknowledged man of genius among the undergraduates. We understood even then that, though barely of age, he was in his own line of inquiry not a beginner but a master. His name was already familiar to men of science. If he lived, it was certain that he would be one of that small but sacred band to whom it would be given to enlarge the bounds of human knowledge. It was a position which might have turned the head of a smaller man; but the friend of whom we were all so proud, and who seemed, as it were, to link us thus early with the great outside world of the pioneers of knowledge, had one of those rich and lavish natures which no prosperity can impoverish, and which makes faith in goodness easy for others.

Another friend – G. W. H. Tayler, who became vicar of Trinity Church, Carlisle – recalled him thus:

We undergraduates felt we had a very uncommon personage amongst us; but we did not then appreciate his rare powers. We had of course heard of the reputation which he had in Edinburgh.

55

But this acute mathematician, so addicted even then to *original* research was among his friends simply the most genial and amusing of companions, the promoter of many a strange theory, the composer of not a few poetic *jeux d'esprits*.

Grave and hard-reading students shook their heads at his discursive talk and reading, and hinted that this kind of pursuits would never *pay* in the long run in the Mathematical Tripos.

I have sometimes watched his countenance in the lecture-room. It was quite a study – there was the look of bright intellect, an entire concentration on the subject, and sometimes a slight smile on the fine expressive mouth, as some point came out clearly before him, or some amusing fancy flitted across his imagination. He used to profess a dislike to reproducing speculations from books, or hearing opinions taken bodily from books.

Yet he read a good deal in other lines than natural philosophy. Sir Thomas Brown's *Religio Medici* was one of his favourite books. Any such author, who propounded his speculations in a quaint, original manner was sure to be a favourite with him.

The youthful Maxwell had a strong streak of idealism. Not that he was ever a rebel – his religious and family roots were too deep. But he did become influenced by F. D. Maurice, a progressive theologian who believed in shouldering some responsibility for his less fortunate brethren in society and is credited with inspiring the Christian Socialist movement. Maurice instituted university courses for 'working men'. Maxwell greatly approved of this and eventually undertook similar work himself – at Cambridge and elsewhere.

Maxwell attended lectures by G. G. Stokes, a man whose contributions to applied mathematics have been of the first rank – as attested by a long list of equations and theorems bearing his name, which pepper any modern basic course in theoretical physics. A quiet and unpretentious man who had little to say outside of his chosen field, he was quickly impressed by Maxwell's talents. Conversely, Maxwell greatly admired him – this was the beginning of a life-long friendship.

Generally speaking Maxwell showed in his choice of friends a predilection for students of theology and future clergymen. Heading a long list of reverends-to-be, of course, was Lewis

Campbell – who was at Oxford, and with whom he kept up a steady correspondence. Others, at Cambridge, were H. M. Butler, G. W. H. Tayler, C. H. Robertson (future Rector of Smeeth) and F. W. Farrar (future Canon of Westminster). Non-ecclesiastically inclined friends were often chosen from fields unconnected with science – like the Irishman R. H. Pomeroy, who took a double degree and was to join the Indian Civil Service, and a handful of fellow-Scots such as Alexander Robertson (C. H.'s brother) and Frank Mackenzie. Two who became intellectual confidants were C. J. Monro, who was a student of mathematics, and R. B. Litchfield who was to found the Working Men's College in London. Most of these are but names to us, their characters and features dim, blurred by the inexorable flow of time. Yet this bare list of itself points to something of importance: it suggests that Maxwell often sought for company and friends outside his circle of fellow mathematics students and future natural philosophers. In his chosen fields, of course, he was far ahead of his coevals and it is likely that, except for a few of the best, they had little to offer him. Besides he thought the scientific mind incomplete and frowned on what he saw as its shallow scepticism. A poem written in 1853 complains 'Pedantry is in demand', and in the autumn of 1851 he writes to Campbell:

> I began a letter last week, but stopped short for want of matter. I will not send you the abortion. Facts are very scarce here. There are little stories of great men for minute philosophers. Sound intelligence from Newmarket for those that put their trust in horses, and Calendristic lore for the votaries of the Senate-house [where the tripos exams took place]. Man requires more. He finds x and y innutricious, Greek and Latin indigestible, and undergrads. nauseous. He starves while being crammed. He wants men's meat, not college pudding. Is truth nowhere but in Mathematics? Is beauty developed only in men's elegant words, or right in Whewell's *Morality*? Must Nature as well as Revelation be examined through canonical spectacles by the dark-lantern of Tradition, and measured out by the learned to the unlearned, all second-hand. I might go on thus. Now do not rashly say I am disgusted with Cambridge and meditating a retreat. On the contrary, I am so engrossed with shoppy things that I have no time to write to you. I am also persuaded

that the study of x and y is to men an essential preparation for the intelligent study of the material universe. That the idea of Beauty is propagated by communication, and that in order thereto language must be and that Whewell's *Morality* is worth reading, if only to see that there *may be* such a thing as a system of Ethics.

That few will grind up these subjects without the help of rules, the awe of authority, and a continued abstinence from unripe realities, etc.

Maxwell clearly did not hold his fellow science students in much esteem. They in turn had reservations about Maxwell – reservations his eccentricity did little to dispel. There were rumours, for instance, that he had discovered a method of throwing cats so that they could not light on their feet and it was said that he demonstrated this by tossing the poor animals out of windows. (When, some twenty years later, the story caught up with him, he was quick to explain that he actually dropped cats on beds and tables from a height of about two inches!) A close friend among undergraduates in mathematics and natural philosophy was P. G. Tait at Peterhouse – who had preceded him from Edinburgh by two years.

It seems likely that Maxwell's straight Scottish Calvinism may also have helped set him apart. In a time of growing sophistication and scepticism, particularly amongst scientifically-minded undergraduates, this was one more factor which may have restricted his choice of friends. His faith seemed altogether uncompromising and rather basic. In a letter to Campbell: 'I believe, with the Westminster Divines and their predecessors *ad Infinitum* that "Man's chief end is to Glorify God and to enjoy him forever." ' And again, a few months later in March 1852:

> You may fly to the ends of the world and find no God but the Author of Salvation. You may search the Scriptures and not find a text to stop you in your explorations.
>
> You may read all History and be compelled to wonder but not to doubt.
>
> Compare the God of Abraham, Issac, and Jacob with the God of the Prophets and the God of the Apostles, and however the Pantheist may contrast the God of Nature with the 'dark Hebrew God', you will find them much liker each other than either like his.

Yet he does attempt to reconcile his faith with his equally deep-seated belief in the importance of free inquiry. In the same letter he expresses himself thus:

> Now, my great plan, which was conceived of old, and quickens and kicks periodically, and is continually making itself more obtrusive, is a plan of Search and Recovery, or Revision and Correction, or Inquisition and Execution, etc. The Rule of the Plan is to let nothing be wilfully left unexamined. Nothing is to be *holy ground* consecrated to Stationary Faith, whether positive or negative. . . . Never hide anything, be it weed or no, nor seem to wish it hidden. So shall all men passing by pluck up the weeds and brandish them in your face, or at least display them for your inspection. . . . Again I assert the Right to Trespass on any plot of Holy Ground which any man has set apart.

This sounds much like science's programme – the credo of the research scientist. Yet what Maxwell has in mind here is religion, an examination of the premises of faith – a broad plan, enough to satisfy the most confirmed agnostic until one gets to this sentence:

> Now I am convinced that no one but a Christian can actually purge his land of these holy spots.

In other words none but a true believer can purge himself of mistaken beliefs. This is a profession of faith which it seems *is* going to be 'wilfully left unexamined'! Maxwell's religious convictions were clearly so deeply imbedded he was unconscious of the inconsistency. Seldom, if ever again, does one catch him in incongruities of this sort. Rather he subscribes, almost, to the fideist view that faith and intellect are separate activities of the mind. As he would put it many years later:

> I think that the results which each man arrives at in his attempts to harmonize his science with his Christianity ought not to be regarded as having any significance except to the man himself, and to him only for a time, and should not receive the stamp of society. For it is of the nature of science, especially of those branches of science which are spreading into unknown regions to be continually . . . [Here the unfinished draft ends; the missing word, one assumes, must imply change.]

Perhaps this is what Maxwell meant when he once said that he had 'no nose for heresy'.

Maxwell's reputation as a youthful scientific genius and the breadth of his interests earned him election to the University's Select Essay Club. This group, which still exists – it was described in a recent *Observer* article as 'an exclusive club of cultural elitists' – consists of twelve members meeting regularly to discuss topical issues; for obvious reasons it was nicknamed *The Apostles*. Many distinguished men have been members – Tennyson, Whitehead, Russell, Maxwell. A number of Maxwell's essays written for the Apostles have survived. Many of these are early efforts to clothe his religious beliefs with logical or scientific argument. Thus his *What is the Nature of Evidence of Design*: 'The belief in design is a necessary consequence of the Laws of Thought acting on the phenomena of perception.' And: 'Every well-ascertained law points to some central cause, and at once constitutes that centre a being in the general sense of the word.'

Maxwell is pursuing here one of theology's chief props on the existence of God. Such dialectics, emanating from a young scientist of outstanding promise, delighted his biographer Lewis Campbell and no doubt other reverends of Maxwell's acquaintance – particularly in view of the growing scepticism of the times. Amongst English and European scientists, the tendency was to reject religion and much of philosophy – a tendency born largely of reaction against extreme attitudes. It was indeed easy to scorn fundamentalist interpretations of the Bible, or the utterances of Archbishop Ussher – who, it will be remembered, fixed the date of creation at 4004 BC. It was natural, too, to laugh at Hegel's pronouncements on the impossibility of there being more than seven planets, a pronouncement made at the turn of the century a few months before the discovery of the minor planet Ceres (Neptune – the ninth planet on this count, but the eighth major one – had been found during Maxwell's adolescence). Maxwell's colleagues took their truths literally; not many, one suspects, had emulated him and attempted to digest Kant in their youth. Having rejected in philosophy, along with the rubbish, much that was valid, they saw themselves as sole custodians of the truth – a view naturally and hotly disputed by philosophers and reverends alike. On both sides there was a widespread tendency to see science and religion as incompatible. Today it is more commonly felt that such arguments are futile; we recognize faith and intellect as complementary – not as congruent categories. But in mid-nineteenth century the issue of science versus religion was very much alive. In Cambridge, in particular, it was a common source of debate and, as a gifted scientist and a profoundly religious man, Maxwell was inevitably stimulated to write and talk on this question. It touched the very core of his thinking; his interest in science had deep philosophical and metaphysical roots. The Oxford philosopher F. H. Bradley could have had Maxwell in mind when in 1893 he said:

> with certain persons, the intellectual effort to understand the universe is a principal way of thus experiencing the Deity. No one, probably, who has not felt this, however differently he might describe it, has ever cared much for metaphysics.

These were intensely busy years for young Maxwell. He kept up an assiduous correspondence with his father, his aunt Jane Cay, Lewis Campbell and sundry friends. He did work on colour theory, optics and geometry. A paper read to the Cambridge Philosophical Society in the spring of 1854 must have been based on work done in 1853; it was entitled *On the Transformation of Surfaces by Bending*. A piece of mathematics deriving from the researches of Gauss, Monge, Liouville and others, this is not yet a great work; but it shows growing mathematical sophistication. And he was certainly doing a lot of preliminary thinking and writing on the theory of electromagnetism which was to bear fruit by 1855. If to this one adds Maxwell's essay-writing for the Apostles and, in the summer and autumn of 1853, his diligent preparation for exams, his level of activity appears to have been remarkable. Yet to his Aunt Jane he writes calmly enough of his studies:

> If any one asks how I am getting on in Mathematics, say that I am busy arranging everything, so as to be able to express it all distinctly, so that examiners may be satisfied now, and pupils edified hereafter. It is pleasant work, and very strengthening, but not nearly finished.

Nevertheless, he overdid it. On a between-terms visit with the Revd C. B. Tayler in Suffolk (the uncle of G. W. H. Tayler), he fell seriously ill. What was described by his host as a 'brain fever' kept him out of circulation for about a month. Whatever the nature of this illness, it was severe enough to make him delirious, helpless and too weak to sit up in bed. The Taylers nursed him like a son, with a kindness and devotion for which Maxwell remained ever grateful – and which, with characteristic religious zest, he was to describe as giving him 'a new perception of the Love of God'.

By mid-summer, Maxwell was back at Cambridge, studying with Hopkins, busy at 'muggery' for the tripos. The exams were held in the Senate-house in January 1854. It is reported that:

> on entering the Senate-house for the first paper he felt his mind almost blank; but by and by his mental vision became preternaturally clear. And, on going out again, he was dizzy and staggering, and was some time in coming to himself.

He came second, i.e. was second wrangler – like his brilliant predecessor W. Thomson. Routh, who was to be a well-known mathematician and dynamicist, came first. At the subsequent examination for the Smith's Prize, regarded as a more serious test of ability, Maxwell shared first place with Routh.

His educational credentials honourably taken care of, Maxwell now had more leisure and possibly better mathematical equipment to pursue his research. He settled down happily to the life of a Cambridge don, a life of scholarship and quiet nights of study. In a letter to his aunt he says:

I am in great luxury here, having but 2 pups., and am able to read the rest of the day, so I have made a big hole in some subjects I wish to know . . . A nightingale has taken up his quarters just outside my window, and works away every night. He is at it very fierce now. At nights the owls relieve him, softly sighing after their fashion.

It was a peaceful time for Maxwell, and a fruitful one. Maxwell was at one with his endeavours; only a happy man could write so:

Happy is the man who can recognise in the work of today a connected portion of the work of life, and an embodiment of the work of Eternity. The foundations of his confidence are unchangeable, for he has been made a partaker of Infinity. He strenuously works out his daily enterprises, because the present is given him for a possession.

He renewed his friendship with his Cay cousins – children of R. Dundas Cay, registrar of the Supreme Court of Hong Kong (from where they had recently returned). Maxwell spent some time with them during this summer holiday in the Lake District near Keswick. Charles Cay was thirteen, interested and gifted in mathematics, as was his elder brother William who, at sixteen, was enrolled at Edinburgh University to study civil engineering.

And there was their sister Elizabeth – Lizzie – then a bright and pretty girl of fourteen (she was born in Edinburgh in April 1840). Maxwell, it appears, was both very fond and deeply attracted to her. Indeed, according to her daughter who was interviewed shortly before her death by C. W. F. Everitt, the feeling was reciprocated and the two were in love. Perhaps it was here in the Peak District, during the summer of 1854, that Maxwell first understood this. One has to assume that in this as in other things Maxwell's thinking would have been individual and idiosyncratic; he may not have seen anything untoward in being in love with a fourteen-year old – besides fifteen and sixteen-year old girls were considered marriageable in those times. We know Maxwell had, in Campbell's words, 'a joyous time' that summer. He actually walked the fifty miles home from Carlisle to Glenlair.

At this age – he was twenty-three – Maxwell was already totally given to his scientific pursuits. It is unlikely that his love for Lizzie had a great influence on the pattern of his life. He pursued, for a while, a presumably passionate correspondence with her. Unfortunately – according, again, to Lizzie's daughter – these letters were burnt. And in all likelihood because of pressure from relatives – motivated by fears of consanguinity – and perhaps due to similar second thoughts on Maxwell's part, the relationship was abandoned. Facts on this are scarce; regrettably, Campbell has shrouded the whole affair under a blanket of genteel, protective silence.

1855 was a hectic year for Maxwell. In February he was kept in Edinburgh, nursing his father abed with bronchitis or pneumonia. James cooked, prepared medicines and draughts and, generally speaking, surrounded his parent with tenderness and care. It was rather remarkable for one so young, so bursting with ideas and creative drive, to have undertaken this labour of love. It shows us, as little else could, the emotional depth of the man. In a letter to a friend, he takes it all lightly enough:

I am at present superintending a course of treatment practised on my father, for the sake of relieving certain defluxions which take place in his bronchial tubes. These obstructions are now giving way, and the medico, who is a skilful bellowsmender, pronounces the passages nearly clear.

However, it will be a week or two before he is on his pins again, so would you have the goodness to tell Freeman to tell Mrs Jones to tell those whom it may concern, that I cannot be up to time at all . . . I have now to do a little cooking and buttling, in the shape of toast and beef-tea and everfizzing draught.

In March Maxwell presented to the Royal Society of Edinburgh a paper on the mixture of colours, entitled *Experiments on Colour, as perceived by the Eye, with remarks on Colour-blindness*. He demonstrated what was then his favourite tool in this field of work: a spinning top with a flat disk-like surface on which he could expose various sized sectors of coloured paper. When the top was spun rapidly, the eye perceived a uniform tint. This showed how any natural colour could be represented by a suitable mixture of three primaries: red, blue and green. The fundamental idea was not new: Young had propounded a similar theory some fifty years earlier and had offered the correct explanation, which is physiological: there are, in most people, three types of receptor cell (cones) in the retina, each sensitive to a particular hue. Maxwell's 1855 paper describes the experimental conditions and rules of colour combination. It is a preliminary study, the origins of which can be traced to work he began in Edinburgh with Forbes: but the latter having fallen seriously ill, Maxwell finished it alone. With Young's earlier work this marks the beginning of modern colorimatry. It is a major paper – Maxwell's first, largely experimental, and a model of thoroughness. He must have put the final touches on it between hours of nursing his sick father.

In October of this same year Maxwell became a fellow of Trinity. And in November he was once again a nursemaid – this time to his friend Pomeroy, his gentle 'Irish giant', ill of 'the bilious fever'. Witnesses stated that he spent hours each day taking care of his patient. At that time he also began to teach working men's evening classes. And he undertook the writing of a textbook on optics for Macmillan – a project which, as he told his father, would involve much work 'and certainly no vain fame, except in Macmillan's puffs'. The plan of the book was novel; he started by assuming it possible to obtain perfect images and then proceeded to investigate the laws of reflection and refraction which will allow this – an approach, says Garnett, 'calculated to bring down a storm of abuse upon the author'. The book was never completed – probably because he was also preparing his great paper *On Faraday's Lines of Force*, the first part of which he would deliver in December before the Cambridge Philosophical Society.

6

FARADAY'S LINES
OF FORCE

For Maxwell 1855 meant the securing of a Trinity fellowship, the illness of his father, intensive reading and the birth of two major scientific works – one on colour, the other on electromagnetism. The former, as mentioned before, established the basis of modern colorimetry; a first-rate piece of work, it was nevertheless no true measure of Maxwell's talent or greatness. The paper on electromagnetism, on the other hand, shows real stirrings of his genius.

On the national and international scenes times were uneasy. Politics were dominated by the Crimean war – the Angel of Death, said John Bright, had been abroad throughout the land. Cables had been laid through Europe and in the Spring of 1855, somewhat to the generals' distress, a telegraphic link had been established between London and the Crimea – incorporating, one must assume, the best of existing electrical devices and W. Thomson's latest improvements. But neither news of the war, nor the political storms surrounding the obscene and useless butchery, made any deep impression on the quiet tenor of Maxwell's life. In his correspondence there is hardly a mention of war or its protagonists. Events and personalities slid by him, like pictures on a silent screen – secondary background to the far more absorbing happenings taking place in the privacy of his mind. For he was already weaving the strands of what would be his greatest work: the theory of electromagnetism, something infinitely more significant and lasting than the contemporary blunderings of monarchs, statesmen or generals. When it was completed in 1864 the theory held the seeds of modern physics, and of Einstein's great work in particular, and of much of our present technology – radar, radio, television. All branches of applied electricity, from the power industry to electronics, have been illumined by it. Few, if any, nineteenth century events would be so pregnant with consequences for the centuries and millenia ahead. And no discovery of that century, with the possible exception of the Darwin-Wallace theory of evolution, is of such intrinsic philosophical interest as Maxwell's work on electromagnetism – the beginnings of which he offered to the Cambridge Philosophical Society meeting in December 1855, under the title of *On Faraday's Lines of Force*.

A necessary attribute of genius is judgement – the ability to lay hand intuitively on that which is truly important, regardless of prevalent opinons or trends. Maxwell, by his early sympathy and interest in Faraday's ideas, an interest dating back to his Edinburgh days, demonstrated this ability to a remarkable degree. In his *Experimental Researches*, Faraday had systematically and elegantly illustrated the concept of *lines of force*. Most people have seen how iron filings can be made to line up in beautiful symmetric curves between the poles of a magnet: these are the lines of magnetic force, or magnetic *field lines*. The force fields generated by electrical charges, by electrical circuits, or by gravitating bodies, also trace patterns of this kind – curves which, at any point in space, show the direction of the acting force. The mind's eye may collect these into tube-like bundles. The strength of the force then varies inversely with the sectional area of the tubes: the tighter and more crowded the lines, the stronger the force and vice versa. Faraday felt these concepts to be more than handy geometrical modes of description. He was convinced that they corresponded to physical properties of the space between the charges or magnetic poles – the space in which these were imbedded. He *knew* that his lines of force allowed a better understanding of electromagnetic phenomena than the traditional idea of forces acting at a distance; but his conviction was not shared by his contemporaries. At the time most physicists thought of forces acting at a distance as the one unassailable fact in the theory of electrical and magnetic phenomena. After all, the attraction of opposite charges and the repulsion between like ones had been thoroughly documented and measured. Coulomb in France had given convincing and elegant experimental demonstrations of the fact that these forces, like Newton's gravitation, varied as the inverse distance squared (1785–90); the point of view had thereby acquired a kind of Newtonian solidity. Poisson, Laplace and others had constructed sophisticated theories based upon these results – an elaborate mathematical edifice which explained many of the observations and measurements dealing with distributions of electrical charge, or magnetic poles, or gravitating masses. W. Thomson had gone a step further and stressed the mathematical analogy – today we call it an isomorphism – between the steady flow of heat in material media and these theories of *static* electric and magnetic fields. All of these were variations on one theme: the paradigm of action-at-a-distance. As far as magneto- and electro-statics were concerned, action-at-a-distance appeared to fit the facts very nicely.

When it came to induction, as when an electric current gives rise to a magnetic field (Ørsted) or a changing magnetic flux induces a current in a conductor, things were less clear. These phenomena, which Faraday had studied for more than twenty years, were not static but *dynamic*. They did not fit so easily into the action-at-a-distance framework. Faraday saw this, but the prevailing climate of opinion was against him – his gropings for a different, unorthodox kind of picture were seen as unnecessary. Action-at-a-distance *had* been a satisfactory, successful model. The remaining problems, it was felt, were largely mathematical: how to calculate the forces between more complex structures, involving moving charges, while starting from this simple and hitherto highly useful hypothesis. And indeed efforts by others, such as Wilhelm Weber in Germany, indicated that this should be possible. Sir George Airy, a true mandarin of Victorian science – astronomer royal, ex-Plumian professor of astronomy at Cambridge, ex-Lucasian professor of mathematics – pronounced himself thus:

> I can hardly imagine anyone (who knows the agreement between observation and calculation based on action at a distance) to hesitate an instant between this simple and precise action on the one hand and anything so vague and varying as lines of force on the other.

Maxwell, nevertheless, was of a different opinion. The simple mechanistic image of forces reaching out somehow across empty space and pushing or pulling at distant charges did not satisfy him. When it came to physical theories, he had a sceptical mind – thanks, at least in part, to the thorough philosophical training he had received in Edinburgh. Never naive enough to believe that science dealt with ultimate truths, he felt always that analogical thinking was the best one could hope for. Science *described* the behaviour of things – no more. There were no compelling reasons why such behaviour should fit our preconceived, physiologically conditioned views of reality. Maxwell's instinct was to reject existing models of electromagnetic phenomena – even when it seemed that a degree of sanction for them could be traced back to Newton himself. He accepted from the start Faraday's intuition concerning the importance of the concept of lines of force, and undertook to interpret this in analogical and mathematical terms. This is what most of Maxwell's first great paper, *On Faraday's Lines of Force*, is about.

P. G. Tait relates that Maxwell showed him a preliminary version of the manuscript already in 1853. The final version was read to the Cambridge Philosophical Society in two sections, on 10 December 1855 and 11 February 1856. In it Maxwell used and enlarged the analogy, sketched earlier by

W. Thomson, between electric or magnetic fields and the steady flow of heat – not before enquiring thoughtfully of Thomson whether he would mind someone 'poaching on his electrical preserves' and receiving an equally gentlemanly assurance that this would be all right (an exchange of courtesies which, alas, strikes one today as quaint).

Maxwell's philosophical turn of mind is much in evidence in this work, as he proceeds to clarify the problems of analogical thinking – without which he always maintained that it would be impossible to understand electricity and magnetism. The very concept of *understanding* in science is difficult to define – for philosophers and laymen alike. Most of us believe we understand a phenomenon when we see it in simple cause and effect relationships between objects accessible to our senses. We *understand* very well that the sun rises and sets because the earth spins on its axis. We *understand* that a rocket moves because of the push of the escaping or exploding propellant on its container. And, after an introductory course in physics, we may understand this in more sophisticated terms as an example of the principle of momentum conservation. These are straightforward phenomena accessible, more or less, to our senses and amenable to our intuition. We *feel* we understand them. Electricity and magnetism, however, are subtly different; except for the special case of light, they are not part of the everyday sensory world. In this respect the physicist does no better than the layman: he too cannot perceive the electromagnetic field. Nature is replete with such examples and much of one's puzzlement at the concepts of modern physics is really unnecessary: the physicist has little more comprehension of electrons, photons or electromagnetism than the non-scientist. He is merely adept at describing and predicting their behaviour through the use of mathematical models or analogies; he is more *used* to these concepts – they are part of the everyday paraphernalia of his thinking and unless he is also a bit of a philosopher, he hardly gives them a thought. But *understand* them he does not – not, that is, in the essential, concrete sense in which he understands the classical Newtonian world of perception. So let not the layman despair at his own difficulties – the scientifically-trained men and women of our technological society hardly do better: they are simply expert in the manipulation of their mathematical models. Maxwell saw that and, in a sense, put it to conscious use in this, his first great article on electromagnetism. Here, as in all his work on the subject, he emphasizes the need to think in *analogies*.

The paper opens masterfully:

The present state of electrical science seems peculiarly unfavourable to speculation. The laws of the distribution of electricity on the surface of conductors have been analytically deduced from experiment; some parts of the mathematical theory of magnetism are established, while in other parts the experimental data are wanting; the theory of the conduction of galvanism and that of the mutual attraction of conductors have been reduced to mathematical formulae, but have not fallen into relation with the other parts of the science. No electrical theory can now be put forth, unless it shows the connexion not only between electricity at rest and current electricity, but between the attractions and inductive effects of electricity in both states. Such a theory must accurately satisfy those laws, the mathematical form of which is known, and must afford the means of calculating the effects in the limiting cases where the known formulae are inapplicable. In order therefore to appreciate the requirements of the science, the student must make himself familiar with a considerable body of most intricate mathematics, the mere retention of which in the memory materially interferes with further progress. The first process therefore in the effectual study of the science, must be one of simplification and reduction of the results of previous investigations to a form in which the mind can grasp them. The results of this simplification may take the form of a purely mathematical formula or of a physical hypothesis. In the first case we entirely lose sight of the phenomenon to be explained; and though we may trace out the consequences of given laws, we can never obtain more extended views of the connexions of the subject. If, on the other hand, we adopt a physical hypothesis, we see the phenomena only through a medium, and are liable to that blindness to facts and rashness in assumption which a partial explanation encourages. We must therefore discover some method of investigation which allows the mind at every step to lay hold of a clear physical conception, without being committed to any theory founded on the physical science from which that conception is borrowed, so that it is neither drawn aside from the subject in pursuit of analytical subtleties, nor carried beyond the truth by a favourite hypothesis.

In order to obtain physical ideas without adopting a physical theory we must make ourselves familiar with the existence of physical analogies. By a physical analogy I mean that partial similarity between the laws of one science and those of another which makes each of them illustrate the other.

These statements must be kept in mind in trying to gauge Maxwell's attitude towards the occasionally bizarre models he will use in later papers. Going on to the specific case of action at a distance, he continues:

There is no formula in applied mathematics more consistent with nature than the formula of attractions, and no theory better established in the minds of men than the action of bodies on one another at a distance. The laws of conduction of heat in uniform media appear at first sight among the most different in their physical relations from those relating to attractions. The quantities which enter them are *temperature, flow of heat, conductivity*. The word *force* is foreign to the subject. Yet we find that the mathematical laws of the uniform motion of heat in homogeneous media are identical in form with those of attractions varying inversely as the square of the distance. We have only to substitute *source of heat* for *centre of attraction, flow of heat* for *accelerating effect of attraction* at any point, and *temperature* for *potential*, and the solution of a problem in attractions is transformed into that of a problem in heat . . . Now the conduction of heat is supposed to proceed by an action between contiguous parts of the medium, while the force of attraction is a relation between distant bodies, and yet, if we knew nothing more than is expressed in the mathematical formulae, there would be nothing to distinguish between the one set of phenomena and the other . . . It is by the use of analogies of this kind that I have attempted to bring before the mind, in a convenient and manageable form, these mathematical ideas which are necessary to the study of the phenomena of electricity. The methods are generally those suggested by the processes of reasoning which are found in the researches of Faraday, and which, though they have been interpreted mathematically by Prof. Thomson and others, are very generally supposed to be of an indefinite and unmathematical character, when compared with those employed by the professed mathematicians. By the method which I adopt, I hope to render it evident that I am not attempting to establish any physical theory of a science in which I have hardly made a single experiment, and that the limit of my design is to shew how, by a strict application of the ideas and methods of Faraday, the connexion of very different orders of phenomena which he has discovered may be clearly placed before the mathematical mind.

Maxwell then suggests that a very good analogy for electric and magnetic lines of force is provided by the motion of a fictitious fluid, with the velocity of the fluid representing the intensity of the force. The fluid he uses is not a real one, for its properties are strange: not only is it incompressible, it is imponderable. Well aware of the oddities of this model, Maxwell produced an analogy which, while seemingly unrealistic and abstract, allowed him to develop an almost physical, sensuous understanding for the behaviour of the field lines. This however was not yet a theory of electromagnetism; as he put it:

> By referring everything to the purely geometrical idea of the motion of an imaginary fluid, I hope to attain generality and precision, and to avoid the dangers arising from a premature theory professing to explain the cause of the phenomena.

And in reference to his mathematical treatment of Faraday's empirical results, Maxwell adds the caveat:

> I do not think that it contains even the shadow of a true physical theory; in fact, its chief merit as a temporary instrument of research is that it does not, even in appearance, *account for* anything.

Maxwell also voices clear doubts concerning the action-at-a-distance viewpoint. Specifically, he is sceptical of Weber's theory which assumed that moving charges acted on each other through a modified Coulomb's law which depends not only on the distance between them, but also on their relative speeds. He refers to it as a 'professedly physical theory of electrodynamics'. But, he adds, 'It is a good thing to have two ways of looking at a subject, and to admit that there *are* two ways of looking at it'. However:

> I do not think that we have any right at present to understand the action of electricity, and I hold that the chief merit of a temporary theory is,

that it shall guide experiment, without impeding the progress of the true theory when it appears. There are also objections to making any ultimate forces in nature depend on the velocity of the bodies between which they act.'

Today one cannot agree with the last sentence – the objections Maxwell had in mind have, ironically, been removed by the consequences of his own theory. Otherwise the development of modern physics has proved him right: the field point of view is both more fundamental and better adapted to the description of electromagnetic phenomena than action-at-a-distance between moving charges. It is also evident to us, in retrospect, that Maxwell is being too modest and conservative in assessing the significance of this, his first paper on electromagnetism. It contains, at the very least, some crucial scaffolding for his final theory.

After showing how, from his analogy, he can reproduce extant results of the theory of electricity and magnetism, Maxwell proceeds to Faraday's idea of an 'electro-tonic state'. Interpreted by Faraday as a kind of tension of the medium in which electromagnetic phenomena are imbedded, it is *not* an observable state. Its *changes* in time and space lead to electrical or magnetic forces, but the electro-tonic state itself cannot be observed or measured. It is actually astonishing that an experimental physicist like Faraday should have arrived at such an idea. Today, under its modern name of vector potential, it is recognized as a powerful unifying and simplifying concept – largely thanks to the manner in which Maxwell used it. By embracing this concept Maxwell, once again, shows a sure touch, foreshadowing his mature views – which would recognize that mechanistic models of electromagnetism are unnecessary. In the meantime, his objectives are modest:

In this outline of Faraday's electrical theories, as they appear from a mathematical point of view, I can do no more than simply state the mathematical methods by which I believe that electrical phenomena can be best comprehended and reduced to calculation, and my aim has been to present the mathematical ideas to the mind in an embodied form, as

74

systems of lines or surfaces, and not as mere symbols, which neither convey the same ideas, nor readily adapt themselves to the phenomena to be explained. The idea of the electro-tonic state, however, has not yet presented itself to my mind in such a form that its nature and properties may be clearly explained without reference to mere symbols, and therefore I propose in the following investigation to use symbols freely, and to take for granted ordinary mathematical operations. By a careful study of the laws of elastic solids and the motions of viscous fluids, I hope to discover a method of forming a mechanical conception of this electro-tonic state adapted to general reasoning.

The insights acquired by Maxwell as an Edinburgh undergraduate five years earlier in his work on the elasticity of solids have not been lost; the connection or *analogy* between stress fields in solids and Faraday's lines of force is clearly on his mind.

In the remainder of the paper Maxwell develops the mathematical relationships between this peculiar electro-tonic state and observable phenomena: this is the last, lengthy, technical portion of the article and is highly mathematical. A year later, having received an offprint, Faraday wrote to Maxwell:

> My Dear Sir,   I received your paper, and thank you very much for it. I do not venture to thank you for what you have said about 'Lines of Force', because I know you have done it for the interests of philosophical truth; but you must suppose it is work grateful to me, and gives me much encouragement to think on. I was at first almost frightened when I saw such mathematical force made to bear upon the subject, and then wondered to see that the subject stood it so well.

With one exception, this is the longest of Maxwell's research papers. He had cause to explain his views at length; he was well aware of the subtlety of the concepts he was formulating and of the resistance they might encounter. Indeed, he wrote concurrently a long essay for the Apostles, entitled *Analogies. Are there Real Analogies in Nature?* While it is unlikely that this contributed much toward making his ideas digestible to his colleagues, it is an interesting effort, in which he explains his philosophy in far more detail than he could in a scientific paper. Thus:

That analogies appear to exist is plain in the face of things, for all parables, fables, similes, metaphors, tropes, and figures of speech are analogies, natural or revealed, artificial or concealed . . . Neither is there any question as to the occurrence of analogies to our minds. They are as plenty as reasons, not to say blackberries. For, not to mention all the things in external nature which men have seen as the projections of things in their own minds, the whole framework of science, up to the very pinnacle of philosophy, seems sometimes a dissected model of nature, and sometimes a natural growth on the inner surface of the mind. Now, if in examining the admitted truths in science and philosophy, we find certain general principles appearing through a vast range of subjects, and sometimes re-appearing in some quite distinct part of human knowledge . . . are we to conclude that these various departments of nature in which analogous laws exist, have a real inter-dependence; or that their relation is only apparent and owing to the necessary conditions of human thought?

. . . The question of the reality of analogies in nature derives most of its interest from its application to the opinion, that all phenomena of nature, being varieties of motion, can only differ in complexity, and therefore the only way of studying nature, is to master the fundamental laws of motion first, and then examine what kind of complication of these laws must be studied in order to obtain true views of the universe. If this theory be true, we must look for indications of these fundamental laws throughout the whole range of science, and not least among those remarkable products of organic life, the results of cerebration (commonly called 'thinking'). In this case, of course, the resemblances between the laws of different classes of phenomena should hardly be called analogies, as they are only transformed identities.

If, on the other hand, we start from the study of the laws of thought (the abstract, logical laws, not the *physio*logical), then these apparent analogies become merely repetitions by reflexion of certain necessary modes of action to which our minds are subject.

Here is the mature development of the epistemological theme he had touched upon earlier in Edinburgh, as a nineteen-year-old undergraduate: our understanding is limited by the very structure of our intellect. The intelligibility of the universe itself is questionable:

Perhaps the 'book', as it has been called, of nature is regularly paged; if so, no doubt the introductory parts will explain those that follow, and the methods taught in the first chapters will be taken for granted and used as illustrations in the more advanced parts of the course; but if it is not a 'book' at all, but a *magazine*, nothing is more foolish to suppose that one part can throw light on another.

In one passage Maxwell is intrigued by the relevance of all this to the classic theological arguments for cosmic design:

> Perhaps the next most remarkable analogy is between the principle, law, or plan according to which all things are made suitably to what they have to do, and the intention which a man has of making machines which will work. The doctrine of final causes, although productive of barrenness in its exclusive form, has certainly been a great help to enquirers into nature; and if we only maintain the existence of the analogy, and allow observation to determine its form, we cannot be led far from the truth.

His final reflection on analogy is this:

> Last of all we have the secondary forms of crystals bursting in upon us, and sparkling in the rigidity of mathematical necessity and telling us, neither of harmony of design, usefulness or moral significance, – nothing but spherical trigonometry and Napier's analogies. It is because we have blindly excluded the lessons of these angular bodies from the domain of human knowledge that we are still in doubt about the great doctrine that the only laws of matter are those which our minds must fabricate, and the only laws of mind are fabricated for it by matter.

Here Maxwell seems to be pleading for a wider use, in science and philosophy, of the concepts of symmetry so dear to the crystallographers. If so, this is prophetic – it foreshadows the uses of group theory, which would be applied to crystals at the end of the nineteenth century and is now a cornerstone of modern particle physics. Perhaps the last sentence is the most interesting: the laws of intellect and matter are inseparable – there is, Maxwell tells us, no objective physics independent of mind. As Eddington would put it, the footprints on the sand are our own.

These thoughts on the uses of analogical thinking give us fair warning: we must not take Maxwell's electromagnetic model-making too much to heart. Models, says he, are fine and useful things, but we must remember that they are the imprint of our minds on an external reality which may be ultimately inaccessible. The fluid analogy in *On Faraday's Lines of Force*, or the outlandish models used by Maxwell in later writings, need not disturb us; he uses them only as aides – for his own thinking and for his readers.

On Faraday's Lines of Force has a peculiar place in the development of Maxwell's thought and in the history of science. In chapter nine I will place this paper, together with his completed theory, in the context of the history of electricity and magnetism. For the moment it is enough to note that, as Maxwell points out, it is not a theory of electromagnetism – not yet. But it is a definite beginning – a platform from which Maxwell will build outwards and upwards in his later work. It shows extraordinary intuition and foresight in that it establishes precisely the kind of scaffolding he was going to need *six years hence*. Maxwell knew exactly, albeit subconsciously, where he was heading. At the same time he would not rush – a remarkable exercise in judgement and perhaps self-control. It is typical of the way Maxwell wrestled with important problems. He first laid the foundations, in a preliminary but thorough study. Some years later, he would come back with a masterful and mature work – for which the first had prepared the ground. He would do this with the theory of colour, with the molecular theory of gases and with his theory of the electromagnetic field.

7

ABERDEEN

Glenlair, Thursday Afternoon, 3rd April 1856.
To Miss Jane Cay.

Dear Aunt,   My father died to-day at twelve o'clock. He was
sleepless and confused at night, but got up to breakfast. He saw Sandy a
few minutes, and spoke rationally, then came into the drawing-room,
and sat down on a chair for a few mintues to rest, and gave a short cry
and never spoke again. We gave him ether for a little, but he could not
swallow it. There was no warning, and apparently no pain. He expected
it long, and described it so himself.

Do you think Uncle Robert could come down and help a little? Tell
Dr. Bell and other people. As it is, it is better than if it had been when I
was away. He would not let me stay. I was to go to Cambridge on
Friday.   Your aff. nephew.

J. C. MAXWELL

Six weeks before, encouraged by Forbes, Maxwell had
applied for the professorship of natural philosophy at the
University of Aberdeen. The academic year in Scottish
universities was short and would leave him freedom to pursue
his research. If he didn't like the job, he could always leave; as
Mr Clerk Maxwell had said: 'If the *postie* be gotten, and prove
not good, it can be given up; at any rate it occupies only half a
year.' More importantly, Aberdeen was nearer home than
Cambridge and Maxwell wanted to stay within reach of his

ailing father. And indeed, cheered by the prospect of seeing more of his son, Mr Clerk Maxwell had briefly responded by taking a turn for the better.

Maxwell's relationship with his father had been unusually close. However, he gave little public show of grief, even to relatives, though he unburdened himself in a pensive if somewhat ponderous poem which he called *Recollections of Dreamland*. Two weeks after his father's death Maxwell returned to Trinity, to complete his duties for the term. On 30 April he received word from Forbes that he had been appointed to the chair of natural philosophy in Marischal College, in Aberdeen. He left Cambridge in early June, after writing to Litchfield:

> The transition state from a man into a Don must come at last, and it must be painful, like gradual outrooting of nerves. When it is done there is no more pain, but occasional reminders from some suckers, tap-roots, or other remnants of the old nerves, just to show what was there and what might have been.

The summer in Glenlair was interrupted by a trip to Belfast, to visit his cousin William Cay, who was studying engineering there with James Thomson (the brother of William Thomson). Charles Cay also came to stay in the autumn. Maxwell's family ties were always strong; at this time his links with the Cays were particularly close. By November, he was in Aberdeen, teaching. After a few months he wrote to Aunt Jane:

> I find everything going very smoothly. I never passed an equal time with less trouble. I have plenty of work but no vexation as yet. In fact, I am beginning to fear that I must get ino some scrape just to put an end to my complacency.

And, after describing some of his duties:

> I had a glorious solitary walk to-day in Kincardinshire by the coast – black cliffs and white breakers. I took my second dip this season. I have found a splendid place, sheltered and safe, with gymnastics on a pole afterwards.

The time of the year was February.

In many ways, Maxwell felt at home here. About a year later, he confided to Campbell:

> As for outward act, no one here seems to think me odd or daft. Some did at Cambridge, but here I have escaped. My rule is to avoid the company of young men whom I do not respect, unless I have the control of them.

Yet, as seen from a late 1857 letter, he did not find the local company very stimulating:

> Gaiety is just beginning here again. Society is pretty steady in this latitude – plenty of diversity, but little of great merit or demerit – honest on the whole, and not vulgar . . . No jokes of any kind are understood here. I have not made one for two months, and if I feel one coming I shall bite my tongue.

He kept up an assiduous correponndence with R. B. Litchfield, a fellow-enthusiast of working men's education and for many years secretary of the London Working Men's College. Maxwell continued holding classes for local working men, as he had in Cambridge. Nevertheless lecturing, whether to university students or to working men, was not his primary interest. Research was his lifeblood; teaching was a duty.

In Aberdeen, and through the rest of his life, Maxwell maintained the work-habits he had acquired as a student – reading and writing late into the night, never relinquishing for long his concentration on whatever had captured his attention. In 1856 he wrote a series of summaries of talks and short papers – about optics, colour, the eye, about tops and on a method of constructing Faraday's lines of force by purely geometrical methods. In 1857 he produced a small brilliant article on the theory of the gyroscope, to illustrate which he had a special top made in Aberdeen. This he took with him to Cambridge, when he came up for his M.A. He exhibited it at a tea-party in his room; in the evening, as his friends were leaving, he had set it spinning. Early next morning, seeing from his window one of them crossing the court towards his rooms, he quickly started up the top and jumped back into bed. Although Maxwell admitted the subterfuge, his top became a legend.

Lesser men could have made respectable careers out of the work he did during this period. Yet when compared to his truly great contributions, Maxwell's publications between 1856 and 1858 were not of the first rank. Much of his attention during this time was focussed on one extremely difficult problem: the stability, i.e. the *viability*, of Saturn's rings.

The rings of Saturn had been known since 1659 when the Dutch astronomer and physicist Christiaan Huygens, using a superior telescope, showed that what Galileo had perceived as a vague excrescence was in fact a ring-like disk surrounding the planet. As telescopes improved, the structure of the ring became visible; by the 1850s it was seen to consist of at least two bright zones separated by a dark band. Some of Europe's best mathematicians, such as Laplace, had studied the problem and, within the framework of Newtonian mechanics, had been unable to determine whether such a structure could actually maintain itself. Theory appeared to suggest that the arrangement was unstable and should destroy itself in short order. Science, then, was faced with a conundrum. Since the rings exhibited no significant change over the years and centuries, they were manifestly stable. *Either* what astronomers saw was impossible within the context of Newton's laws and these were invalid in the outer reaches of the solar system, *or* the studies of the great Laplace were incomplete or incorrect.

In March 1855 a Cambridge board of examiners consisting of W. Thomson and two prominent astronomers announced the subject for the fourth Adams Prize: the Motions of Saturn's Rings and, in particular, the question of their stability. The issue seems to have fired Maxwell's imagination and challenged his intuition. As he put it some years later, in the introduction to his final article on the subject:

There are some questions in Astronomy, to which we are attracted rather on account of their peculiarity, as the possible illustration of some unknown principle, than from any direct advantage which their solution would afford to mankind . . . When we contemplate the Rings from a purely scientific point of view, they become the most remarkable bodies in the heavens, except, perhaps, those still less *useful* bodies – the spiral nebulae. When we have actually seen the great arch swung over the equator of the planet without any visible connexion, we cannot bring our minds to rest. We cannot simply admit that such is the case, and describe it as one of the observed facts of nature, not admitting or requiring an explanation. We must either explain its motion on the principles of mechanics, or admit that, in the Saturnian realms, there can be motion regulated by laws which we are unable to explain.

From 1856 to 1858 a large fraction of Maxwell's energies went into this work. His letters are full of references to Saturn; the most graphic is in an August 1857 letter to Campbell:

I have been battering away at Saturn, returning to the charge every now and then. I have effected several breaches in the solid ring, and am now splash into the fluid one, amid a clash of symbols truly astounding. When I reappear it will be in the dusky ring, which is something like the state of the air supposing the siege of Sebastopol conducted from a forest of guns 100 miles one way, and 30,000 miles the other, and the shot never to stop, but go spinning away round a circle, radius 170,000 miles.

The reference to Sebastopol is curious; it is the only explicit reference to the Crimean war in his letters.

The final monograph, published in 1859 and titled *On the Stability of the Motion of Saturn's Rings*, is monumental – ninety quarto pages of mathematics and carefully polished prose. In it Maxwell confirmed that solid rings were impossible and proved that the actual rings had to consist of many small independent bodies – a result verified in modern astronomical and space studies, although the bodies are more variable than Maxwell thought, ranging from metre-sized chunks to boulders a hundred metres in diameter. Recent results obtained by Voyager spacecraft show a much more elaborate structure – consisting of hundreds of rings – than was known to Maxwell. The broad lines of his proof, nevertheless, are still valid. Interestingly, it has been shown recently that Jupiter and Uranus too exhibit diffuse rings: such structures are not as exceptional as was once thought. Maxwell demonstrated that disturbances of the rings propagate as waves; the study of these oscillations leads to the proper stability criteria. It was a brilliant accomplishment – a bravura performance which, perhaps more than anything he had yet published, made him a star in the eyes of his contemporaries. Sir George Airy was to call it 'one of the most remarkable applications of Mathematics to Physics that I have ever seen'. For this work Maxwell received the Adams Prize.

Maxwell's paper *On Faraday's Lines of Force* had already shown the golden touch – the mark of genius. The investigation of Saturn's rings was more a technical triumph; it proved his total mastery of his instrument. And remarkable as it may have been, it is, in the history of scientific ideas, less significant than his great works on electromagnetism or statistical mechanics. There is in fact some evidence that Maxwell's mind bridled at times against the endless calculations entailed in this study. During the summer of 1856, for instance, he writes to Litchfield, telling him that he is working on Saturn's rings, which he finds 'a stiff subject but curious' and adds: 'I find I get fonder of metaphysics and less of calculation continually'.

Maxwell's thoughts were indeed never far from what he saw as the fundamental issues – physical or metaphysical. His interest in the roots of knowledge continued unabated, and takes an interesting turn when he records some views on the origins of his insights. In his *Recollections of Dreamland* he put it this way:

> There are powers and thoughts within us, that we
> know not, till they rise
> Through the stream of conscious action from where the
> Self in secret lies.

But when Will and Sense are silent, by the thoughts
that come and go
We may trace the rocks and eddies in the hidden depths
below

A year later, in a letter to Litchfield, he said it more succinctly: 'I believe there is a department of the mind conducted independent of consciousness, where things are fermented and decocted, so that when they are run off they come clear.' On his deathbed he went even further: what is done by 'what is called myself is, I feel, done by something greater than myself in me.'

Maxwell is not unique among scientists in having observed in himself the workings of subconscious or 'irrational' processes of discovery. Amongst better known accounts of the strange ways of creativity is one by the great French mathematician Henri Poincaré, who described how he arrived at a famous result in these terms:

> contrary to my custom, I drank black coffee and could not sleep. Ideas rose in crowds. I felt them collide until pairs interlocked, so to speak, making a stable combination. By the next morning I had established the existence of a class of Fuchsian functions . . . I had only to write out the results, which took but a few hours.

There is also the classic story of the German chemist Kekule, who hit upon the ring structure of benzene – one of the great breakthroughs of nineteenth-century chemistry – after seeing, in a daydream, the image of a snake swallowing its tail.

Historians of science have tended to regard these great men's accounts of their mental processes as aberrations – curious, subjective anecdotes to be used for entertaining their readers or to be disparaged, depending upon the particular psychological, epistemological or even political views they espoused. Psychologists themselves are divided on the matter, with behaviourists rejecting such tales as irrelevant and depth psychologists welcoming them as very significant. Philosophers, on the other hand, have tended to ignore them. Yet, in describing the ways of science, attention should surely be given to the manner in which some of its greatest practitioners have reached remarkable results. But then if thinking can be carried on by unconscious processes, the subject acquires an uncomfortably anarchic cast – making the logician's or epistemologist's task very difficult, if not impossible. However, there is amongst modern philosophers of science a new school which disputes the very existence of a scientific method; Feyerabend's book *Against Method*, with its aphorism *anything goes*, is a case in point. While Maxwell may never have pushed the matter quite so far, it is perfectly clear that he ascribed an important function to processes beyond the ken of simple reason.

The summer of 1857 was uneventful. Maxwell spent it, as usual, in Glenlair, tending his estate and working – mostly on 'Saturn and his Rings'. Occasionally, he socialized with the gentry. This led to an amusing sketch in a letter to Campbell. It shows humour, observation, real literary merit and gives us a clear-eyed view of local society:

> Old Greenlaw, heir of entail, with charters in his bedroom belonging to 'Young Lochinvar' his forebear, and various Douglases, with rights of pits and gallows, and other curious privileges, sending all his people and visitors neck and heels in the very best direction for themselves. Son and daughter – mild, indefatigable, generally useful, doing (at home) exactly as they are bid. One gay litter(ar)y widow, charming never so wisely, with her hair about her ears and her elbows on her knees, on a low stool, talking Handel, or Ruskin, or Macaulay, or general pathos of unprotected female, passing off into criticism, witticism, pleasantry, unmitigated slang, sporting and betting.
>
> One little Episcopal chaplain, a Celt, whom I see often, but do not quite fathom – that is, I don't know how far he respects and how far he is amused with his most patronising friends. One, mathematical teacher somewhere, – friend of chaplain. Voice. Mild, good fellow, like a grown up chorister, quite modest about everything except his voice – 'What will they say in England', The Standard Bearer', 'Oh Susannah' (Chaplain leads chorus), 'Courtin down in Tenessee' (Chaplain obligato), 'Yet once more' (Handel), 'But who may abide' (do.) and so on.
>
> One good old widow lady, with manners. One son to do., – sanguine

temperament, open countenance, very much run to nose, brain inactive, probably fertile in military virtue. Two daughters to do., – healthy, physical force girls, brains more developed owing to their not having escaped in the form of nose.

Now, conceive the Voice set down beside one of the physical forces, and trying to interest her in the capacities of different rooms for singing in, she being more benevolent and horsefleshy than technically musical, – the Chaplain entertaining the other with an account of his solitary life in his rooms, – old Greenlaw hospitably entreating the mannerly widow, and trying to get the nose to talk.

The young widow fixed on Colin, and informed him that if Solomon were to reappear with all his wisdom, as well as his glory, he would yet have to learn the polka; and that the mode of feasting adopted by the Incas of Peru reminded her strongly of a custom prevalent among the Merovingian kings of France.

Living in the Pampas she regarded as an enviable lot, and she was at a loss to know the best mode of studying Euclid for the advantage of being able to teach a young brother of six (years old) . . .

The Colin referred to was Maxwell's cousin, Colin Mackenzie, who no doubt was staying with him at the time.

In September, upon returning from a holiday in the Highlands, Maxwell learnt of the death of his friend Pomeroy in India during the Great Mutiny. From the lengthy correspondence that ensued it is clear that he was much saddened. Throughout that autumn he mentions and discusses the tragedy in letters to Litchfield, Aunt Jane, C. J. Monro – a mutual friend from the Cambridge years. His words to Litchfield show how deeply he valued his friendships:

> It is in personal union with my friends that I hope to escape the despair which belongs to the contemplation of the outward aspect of things with human eyes. Either be a machine and see nothing but 'phenomena' or else try to be a man, feeling your life interwoven, as it is, with many others, and strengthened by them whether in life or death.

These years were important ones for Maxwell. It was a period during which he matured. He knew grief and a large measure of loneliness. To invert the words he had used in an earlier letter to Litchfield these years marked, for better or for worse, his transition to a man.

The most crucial event in Maxwell's private life during the Aberdeen years was his marriage to Katherine Mary Dewar – the daughter of the principal of Marischal College. On 18 February 1858 he announced his betrothal in a letter to Aunt Jane in these terms:

DEAR AUNT   This comes to tell you I am going to have a wife.
I am not going to write out a catalogue of qualities, as I am not fit; but I can tell you that we are quite necessary to one another, and understand each other better than most couples I have seen.
Don't be afraid; she is not mathematical; but there are other things besides that, and she certainly won't stop the mathematics . . .
So now you know who it is, even Katherine Mary Dewar (hitherto). I have heard Uncle Robert speak (second-hand) of her father, the Principal. Her mother is a first-rate lady, very quiet and discreet, but has stuff in her to go through anything in the way of endurance . . . So there is the state of the case. I settled the matter with her, and the rest of them are conformable.
I hope some day to make you better acquainted . . . For the present you must just take what I say on trust. You know that I am not given to big words. So have faith and you shall know.

Our information on Katherine is scanty and what we learn may well be biased, for she does not seem to have been popular. Campbell's biography appeared during her lifetime and he could not expand upon the subject. In fact Campbell tells us essentially nothing about her; this in itself is suspect – his style is normally expansive and had he been charmed he would have let us know. He confines himself instead to generalities about Maxwell's sterling qualities as a husband – telling us, for instance, that 'his married life . . . can only be spoken of as one of unexampled devotion'. Katherine was seven years older than Maxwell, fair, somewhat taller than him, rather plain. In later years feelings towards her amongst Maxwell's colleagues would be decidedly mixed. There is little doubt that she became neurotic. However, it is most likely that she was not so when Maxwell met her, for while his experience of women was slight he was, nevertheless, a good observer. At the time of their marriage she was thirty-four years old – in Victorian terms, a spinster: but then his father, too, had married a woman of similar years. The letter to Aunt Jane suggests that Maxwell had a foreboding that Katherine might not impress his relatives – as apparently she did not. No doubt there was a feeling James could have done better for himself. Katherine knew of the Elizabeth affair and remained ever jealous of the Cay family. The Cays in turn rather looked down on her. On this marriage Maxwell's aunt, Mrs Wedderburn, pronounced herself cryptically: 'James', she said, 'has lived hitherto at the gate of heaven.'

Of the bethrothal and courtship, of Maxwell's private deliberations, again we know little. But, as was his wont at turning points in his life, he put some of his feelings in verse.

> Will you come along with me,
>   In the fresh spring-tide,
> My comforter to be
>   Through the world so wide?
>
> .   .   .
>
> And the life we then shall lead
>   In the fresh spring-tide,
> Will make thee mine indeed,
>   Though the world be wide.

It is in this poem that Maxwell comes closest to expressing passion. Passion was an emotion he obviously viewed with suspicion. His letters to Katherine contain curious admonitions concerning the flesh – as when he writes to her from Hampshire, where he travelled to be best man at Lewis Campbell's wedding:

> the desire of the spirit is contrary to the desire of the flesh, the one tending towards God, and the other towards the elements of the world, so that we are kept stretched as it were, and this is our training in this life . . .

And later that month:

> What a description of Christ in the last verse, over 'all things' and our vile bodies among the rest, and what a day it will be when He has done all His work and is satisfied.

There is little doubt that Maxwell's upbringing, his Calvinism, the times he lived in, conspired to make him prudish and conservative. His *social* conservatism is revealed in a letter to Katherine from the same period,

> If we despise these relations of marriage, of parents and children, of master and servant, everything will go wrong, and there will be confusion as bad as in Lear's case. But if we reverence them, we shall even see beyond their first aspect a spiritual meaning, for God speaks to us more plainly in these bonds of our life than in anything we can understand. So we find a great deal of Divine Truth is spoken of in the Bible with reference to these three relations and others.

It seems, then, that his attitude towards those less fortunate than himself, whilst benign, was effectively feudal. He felt a strong sense of responsibility for such people – witness his lectures to working men and his interest in Maurice's Christian socialism. Yet he felt that the social order was given to man from above. Outside his scientific work Maxwell had no revolutionary leanings. He accepted the values and the religion handed down to him by his family. In this he stands in stark contrast to other men of science, and particulary to Einstein who, as a member of a historically persecuted minority, vulnerable in a world of swift change and monstrous social and military conflicts, had rebelled already as a boy. Maxwell had been protected and busy, too preoccupied while still a child with his private world of intellect, to have felt exposed or feel threatened by the realities of life. Adolescence – the age at which many of us feel the stirrings of rebellion – had, in a sense, passed him by. And so he settled, at an early age, on a course which neither disturbed his religious beliefs nor raised any urgent questions about the society in which he lived. And he married a woman who, very likely, would disturb neither his work nor his views.

The marriage took place on the second of June 1858, in Aberdeen. There is, in the archives of Trinity College, a brief letter from Maxwell to Lizzie, dated 27 May, telling her of the arrangements that had been made for her – and other members of the Cay family – to attend the ceremony. Had one not known of his earlier feeling for her, it might have struck one as a perfectly ordinary letter to a member of the family. It shows no particular signs of having been laboured over or of having been difficult to write. But two sentences catch the eye: 'I am sorry you have not been well and I only hope this business of mine will do you no harm.' and: 'We are all very well and Katherine thinks she and you are sure to agree.'

Circumstantial evidence suggests a cooling between the Clerk Maxwells and the Cays; agreement, if any, did not last. There are, after this date, no more confiding letters to Aunt Jane. If Maxwell was aware of friction, he did not let it interfere with his life – which would henceforth be, as Campbell put it, one of unexampled husbandly devotion.

During that summer there was a short period in Glenlair during which Maxwell did little – preferring, in his own words, 'the passive enjoyments of sun, wind and streams'. But he was soon back at work, revising and polishing his work on Saturn and pursuing new and exciting thoughts.

It was natural that Maxwell's model of Saturn's rings – clouds of particles, like the canonballs of some nightmarish bombardment – led him to think of gases. A hundred years earlier Daniel Bernouilli had already proposed that a gas – any gas – consisted of immense numbers of minute particles – molecules or atoms – flying about in all directions. He saw them as bumping into each other, continually changing course – 'like people hustled in a crowd', as Maxwell would put it someday – and colliding with the walls of the container. The force of these collisions produces pressures which can be observed and measured and depend upon the volume and temperature in the container. The number of particles involved, though, is astronomical; any description of the gas starting from the mechanics of individual particles is out of the question. In the spring of 1859 Maxwell came across two recent articles by Clausius which suggested that if one used suitable mathematical averaging procedures this seemingly impossibly complex problem could be treated simply. It will be remembered that, as an Edinburgh undergraduate, Maxwell had already concluded that our knowledge of the world is at best probabilistic; after reading Clausius, he offered a simple intuitive mathematical argument giving the probability for a molecule to have a range of velocities – a classic formula known today as the *Maxwell distribution*. This approach was of course founded upon certain assumptions, one of which said that the velocities of particles in the three spatial directions were independent of each other – a hypothesis Maxwell regarded as dubious. Nevertheless, the results were startlingly simple, elegant and in fair agreement with observation; in 1859 Maxwell wrote them into a landmark paper titled *Illustrations of the Dynamical Theory of Gases*. In it he spelt out the inadequacies and assumptions of the theory – such as a modest error in the prediction of the specific heat of gases. He stressed also a new and rather startling prediction of the theory: the viscosity of a gas should be independent of its density. This, he pointed out, was an unexpected result and would some day have to be checked experimentally.

This paper introduced, for the first time in the history of physics, a probabilistic – i.e. a basically indeterministic – view of matter which would, henceforth, become and remain a cornerstone of theoretical physics. It also laid the ground for developments which were to lead eventually to the modern understanding of matter. This was Maxwell's first sortie into the field; his later investigations are more masterful. It is the first stage of a build-up – a platform from which he begins operations in a field he will profoundly change. It was, in his mind, a preliminary. Nevertheless, it marked the opening of a new era in physics – of which more later.

Also in 1859 Maxwell completed his chief opus on colour, *On the Theory of Colour Vision*, which he presented to the Royal Society in London in March 1860. This work, the most comprehensible to his scientific contemporaries, is the least original of his major lines of research. It is founded on Thomas Young's idea that colour sensations can be analyzed in terms of three primary colours – i.e. *any* colour perceived by the human eye is a superposition of these. Young had taken these to be red, green and violet. Maxwell took red, green and blue. Combining then some very simple mathematics with beautifully designed experiments, using his wife as an observer, he established the properties of the fundamental colours – which had to be added or subtracted from each other to produce any desired hue.

The year 1859 was a seminal one for both science and technology. It saw the publication of Darwin's *Origin of Species*. In the ensuing storm, Maxwell's friend and colleague W. Thomson became chief spokesman for 'the physicists', arguing against 'the geologists' that calculations on the cooling rate of a primeval molten Earth *proved* that the span of time available for the evolution of species was inadequate – perhaps by a factor of a hundred. It was a long and bitter argument, which troubled Darwin greatly, and which would only be settled after his death – in his favour – by the discovery of radioactivity: this provided a source of internal heat which, in effect, had kept the planet warm through the eons. In public, at least, Maxwell stayed aloof from the argument. A few indirect allusions here and there, in letters or even in verse, suggest that he was reluctant to accept the theory. One assumes, though, that his intuition made him cautious of taking sides as a scientist in arguments of great complexity, many of which were outside his field. Contrary to what has sometimes been stated, Maxwell had little intellectual arrogance. He was better than most of his colleagues, and he clearly knew it. But he understood the limitations of intellect – also better than most of his colleagues.

On the technological front, the first telegraph message had just been transmitted across the Atlantic, thanks to a cable and sensitive apparatus designed by W. Thomson. This particular triumph was temporarily endangered when, after a few months, the cable parted. In connection with this Maxwell delivered himself of a few couplets entitled 'The Song of the Atlantic Telegraph Company':

> Under the sea
> No little signals are coming to me,
> Under the sea,
> Something has surely gone wrong,
> And it's broke, broke, broke;
> What is the cause of it does not transpire,
> But something has broken the telegraph wire
> With a stroke, stroke, stroke,
> Or else they've been pulling too strong.

It is not recorded whether W. Thomson thought these verses amusing.

The end of Maxwell's Aberdeen appointment was curious. At the age of twenty-nine Maxwell had, as a scientist, reached the full power of his talents. His greatest work was still to come. But he had already written several major papers – on colour, on Saturn's rings, on electromagnetism, on statistical mechanics – all trail-blazing, all touched with genius or, at least, with unique talent. Yet at this point, in 1860, the University of Aberdeen chose to fuse its two colleges, Marischal and Kings, and in doing so eliminate Maxwell's post and make him redundant. There was a peculiar aspect to his dismissal. After fusion there would have been in most cases two professors for every post; the ground rules were that the senior man was to be dismissed (the idea being that, after retirement, the senior man would have received a pension and the college would have been getting less for its money!). In Maxwell's case, however, the rule was broken and the senior man – one David Thomson, nicknamed 'Crafty' – was retained. 'Dafty' lost.

There was perhaps no one in Aberdeen of sufficient calibre to appreciate Maxwell's greatness. It *was* a backwater, and Maxwell knew it. That, however, could hardly excuse his treatment by the university; to let a world-class genius like Maxwell go merely because of some administrative reorganization and internal academic politicking seems outrageous. Maxwell, always self-contained, took his dismissal in stride – with a smile, no doubt, and a quip; there is no record of his having complained about it. The truth is, he may have been getting a bit tired of Aberdeen. They did not appreciate his work; worse yet, they did not understand his jokes.

8

LONDON: FRUITFUL YEARS

Peter Guthrie Tait was in his day a scientist of repute and a member of that remarkable trio of Scotsmen – Maxwell, Thomson, and Tait – who, with English colleagues like Stokes, Rayleigh, and Airy brought British physics to the centre of the world stage. Tait had been a year behind Maxwell at the Edinburgh Academy and had excelled as a student in all subjects, particularly in mathematics. Common interest had drawn the boys together and they became fast friends – exchanging manuscripts and ideas while still at the Academy, competing for prizes and posing maths problems to each other. Yet they were very different – physically and temperamentally. Tait was tall and athletically built with strong, almost brutal features and an expression of heavy concentration. In contrast to Maxwell, whose mind was intuitive and philosophical, Tait's interests lay in problem-solving and in the investigation of mathematical methods. As a technician and as a teacher he was very good indeed. He was thorough, articulate, and had a remarkable presence. One student spoke with awe of the power of his personality: 'I have seen a man fall back in alarm under Tait's eyes, though there were a dozen benches between them.' In his student years Tait, unlike Maxwell, drew little satisfaction from the philosophical approach to education prevailing in Scotland and, after a year at the University of

Edinburgh, he left for Cambridge. Maxwell, on the other hand, spent three years in Edinburgh, assimilating the lectures of Sir William Hamilton and acquiring thereby much insight into philosophical and epistemological questions – a far deeper insight, in fact, than that of his scientific contemporaries. After arriving in Cambridge Maxwell found himself two years behind Tait who in 1852 passed his tripos *con brio* as first wrangler.

In later years Maxwell and Tait kept up a steady correspondence. Dealing largely with technicalities of one sort or another, most of it is of little interest to the non-scientist. Nevertheless it tells us something about the two men. It makes it clear that Maxwell always maintained an honest respect for Tait's mastery of the techniques of their trade. It offers also a glimpse of the camaraderie between them. As the correspondence evolved, there was much on the classic Thomson and Tait *Treatise on Natural Philosophy* – the first part of which appeared in 1867 – wherein Thomson is referred to as T and Tait as T', and the treatise itself as T & T'. Maxwell begins many a missive to Tait as O T'! Another colleague whose name occasionally creeps into the correspondence, John Tyndall – whom Tait disliked – is referred to as T''; Tait liked to refer to him as a second-order quantity. By some vagary of notation one finds in a work by Tait a thermodynamical equation containing Maxwell's initials, reading JCM=dp/dt. Never one to let slip the chance of a joke, Maxwell took to signing his cards and letters as dp/dt. A less arcane witticism stemmed from another gratuitous coincidence: in the 1860s the Archbishops of York and Canterbury were also called Thomson and Tait. Maxwell began referring to his two colleagues as *The Archiepiscopal Pair* – an apt label for two men whose position in nineteenth century British physics was so prominent.

In 1860 Maxwell and Tait both applied for the Edinburgh chair of natural philosophy, from which Forbes had retired. Tait was chosen. According to an article in the *Edinburgh*

Courant, the university curators readily acknowledged Maxwell's pre-eminence as a scientist:

> It will be no disrespect to the warmest friends of the successful candidate, and we do not mean to dispute the decision of the curators, by saying, that in Professor Maxwell the curators would have had the opportunity of associating with the University one who is already acknowledged to be one of the remarkable men known to the scientific world. His original investigations on the nature of colours, on the mechanical condition of stability of Saturn's rings, and many similar subjects, have well established his name among scientific men . . . But there is another power which is desirable in a professor of a University with a system like ours, and that is, the power of oral exposition proceeding upon the supposition of a previous imperfect knowledge, or even total ignorance, of the study on the part of the pupils. We little doubt that it was the deficiency of this power in Professor Maxwell principally that made the curators prefer Mr Tait.

Evidently it was common knowledge that Maxwell was a poor teacher. A student and biographer of Tait's – C. G. Knott – states that Maxwell was 'curiously lacking . . . in the power of oral exposition' whereas Tait, as a lecturer, 'was probably unsurpassed by any of his contemporaries'.

Undeterred by this rebuff Maxwell applied for the vacant chair of physics and astronomy at King's College, London, and was quickly accepted in July 1860. Even so his path to London was not a smooth one. Towards the end of the summer Maxwell went to a fair near Glenlair, to buy a horse. A week or so later he became violently sick, with high fever and headache. The illness was diagnosed as smallpox, contracted in all likelihood at the fair – by no means a rare disease in those times. For some days Maxwell hovered at death's door. Isolated in a section of the house, Katherine read him the bible and ministered to his needs. In later years Maxwell always stressed that she had saved his life.

He recovered fully, and in the autumn the Maxwells moved to London – into a new, comfortable four-storeyed house at 8 Palace Gardens Terrace in Kensington. (It still stands, its number now changed to 16.) The Maxwells did not buy it, but leased it from the Kensington Church Commissioners. The location had been carefully chosen: it was within reasonable walking distance from the college and available close by was a horse-drawn bus service. Most importantly, the park was near, allowing regular afternoon horseback riding. James and Katherine were ardent and expert riders; they brought with them from Glenlair Katherine's favourite horse Charlie – a high-bred light Galloway. Here Maxwell settled down to some of the busiest and most creative years of his life.

The teaching load was heavier than it had been at Aberdeen; the academic terms were longer and the pupils more numerous. But then, as now, the professor's lot was not overly harsh: Maxwell had approximately six hours of classes per week, and yearly holidays of about four months. He had plenty of time for research and writing. Nevertheless a lecturer was appointed to help Maxwell with his courses. From 1863 on this was W. G. Adams, the brother of John Couch Adams of Neptune fame – an able young man who would eventually inherit Maxwell's chair. C. Domb, in a study of college records shows that Maxwell took great care in selecting and ordering the material for his courses. Their conception and organization were modern in spirit, covering mechanics, optics, electricity and magnetism. Maxwell was not a good teacher and there are intimations that he did not keep order in his classes very well, but he was conscientious, meticulous and well-organized in the preparation of his lectures. There is little doubt however that lecturing frustrated him. Thus in a 1862 letter to Campbell, who was not teaching at the time:

> I hope you enjoy the absence of pupils. I find that the division of them into smaller classes is a great help to me and to them: but the total oblivion of them for definite intervals is a necessary condition for doing them justice at the proper time.

Few modern professors will admit to wishing for the total oblivion of their students; yet all must at some time indulge in such dreams in one form or another. In Maxwell's case such hopes would have been especially understandable. The evidence is that, as a teacher, he had unusual difficulties. His delivery was poor. He could control neither the speed of his thought nor the flights of his mind. He tended to pursue sidelines – sudden inspirations, which took him in unpredictable directions. He made mistakes. As Horace Lamb, a later junior colleague at Cambridge, would put it 'he had his full share of misfortunes at the blackboard'. Very likely only the occasional, particularly brilliant student could follow his lectures.

A sample of Maxwell's pedagogical outlook crops up in the avuncular advice he vouchsafed to young Charles Cay, who was teaching mathematics at Clifton College:

> I hope you keep your conscience in good order, and do not bestow more labour on erroneous papers than is useful to the youth who wrote it. Always set him to look for the mistake, if he prefers that to starting fresh, for to find your own mistake may sometimes be profitable, but to seek for another man's mistake is weariness to the flesh.
>
> There are three ways of learning props – the heart, the head, and the fingers; of these the fingers is the thing for examinations, but it requires constant practice. Nevertheless the fingers have a fully better retention of methods than the heart has. The head method requires about a mustard seed of thought, which, of course, is expensive, but then it takes away all anxiety. The heart method is full of anxiety, but dispenses with the thought, and the finger method requires great labour and constant practice, but dispenses with thought and anxiety together.

– skimpy and enigmatic advice, surely, for a young teacher. What it actually shows is Maxwell's appreciation of the main requirements for scientific creativity: intuition (heart), reason (head) and technique (fingers). As a great scientist, an honest man, and a dutiful teacher he would dearly have liked to transfer his own mastery of these ingredients to his students; but his success at this remained at all times erratic.

Maxwell regularly attended sessions at the Royal Institution, where he must have often met Faraday. One day, after attending a lecture there, he found himself trapped in the slow-moving crowd heading for the exit. Faraday, similarly wedged and unable to do more than let himself be carried by the current, spotted him from a distance. Familiar with Maxwell's work on the kinetic theory of gases – which involved modelling a gas by means of large numbers of colliding molecules – he shouted: 'Ho, Maxwell, can't you get out? If any man can find his way through a crowd, it should be you!'

Maxwell and Faraday dined together on the day of Maxwell's famous 1861 lecture at the Royal Institution. Their relationship was always cordial. Maxwell stood in awe of Faraday's talents; of all his contemporaries, he understood best the significance of Faraday's results, and the depth of his thought. Conversely, Faraday greatly admired Maxwell's grasp of electromagnetic theory. Their work complemented each other's perfectly; they were natural intellectual allies at a time when their *field* views on electromagnetism were not generally accepted. Yet there is no record of any close friendship between them. Neither was sociable, their backgrounds were very different and there was between them an age gap of forty years. Besides, Faraday was at that point suffering some mental and physical deterioration, due probably to mercury poisoning (mercury baths were commonly in use in laboratories to establish dependable electrical connections). Faraday's religious views may also have seemed eccentric to Maxwell: he was an elder of the tiny sect of Sandemanians which believed, among other things, that to accumulate property was evil, forbade marrying outside the faith, and made attendance at all prayer meetings compulsory.

In 1861 Maxwell became a fellow of the Royal Society. His friend Tait never made it – despite the fact that there were, on the rosters of this august body, many less distinguished, now long-forgotten names. It is said that the President of the Royal Society did approach Tait in 1880 but, at this point, he replied rather haughtily that he did not wish to belong to a Society that was too good for a friend of his who had just been rejected.

The Maxwells' lives in London were uneventful. Relatives visited, although this is unlikely to have happened often – despite good train service, the journey from Scotland was not undertaken lightly in those days. Katherine's brother, the Revd Donald Dewar, came to London to undergo an operation at the hands of a well-known surgeon. Maxwell not only gave up the use of his ground floor to his brother-in-law, but personally helped nurse him. Compassion and patience combined to make him an excellent nurse. The patient, Campbell reports, used to await Maxwell's return from the college with almost childlike expectation.

Contact with the Cays – or, at least, with male members of the family – was kept up through the 1860s. Charles Cay, in particular, remained a favourite and spent much time at Glenlair during the holidays. So did his brother William; now a professional engineer, he was hired by Maxwell to build a stone bridge across the Urr. The bridge, of traditional sturdy design, is still there; it has stood up well to the weather and the onslaughts of the often flood-swollen, fast-flowing river.

Maxwell's relationship with Katherine during these early years of marriage appears to have been harmonious enough and, like the rest of his dealings with mankind, uneventful. When separated from her by the exigencies of work and travel, he wrote faithfully and at length. But the letters, or at least the passages quoted by Campbell, sound strange to the modern ear. Thus, on 13 April 1860:

> Now let us read (c Cor.) chapter xii., about the organization of the Church, and the different gifts of the different Christians, and the reason of these differences that Christ's body may be more complete in all its parts. If we felt more distinctly our union with Christ, we would know our position as members of his body, and work more willingly and intelligently along with the rest in promoting the health and growth of the body, by the use of every power which the spirit has distributed to us.

And on 22 June 1864:

> May the Lord preserve you from all evil, and cause all the evil that assaults you to work out His own purposes, that the life of Jesus may be made manifest in you, and may you see the eternal weight of glory

behind the momentary lightness of affliction, and so get your eyes off things seen and temporal, and be refreshed with the things eternal! Now love is an eternal thing, and love between father and son or husband and wife is not temporal if it be the right sort . . .

Letters in a similar vein are dated 23, 26, and 28 June. Victorian convention made it difficult for people to talk or think forthrightly about intimate aspects of their lives. We are left to speculate whether some hidden crisis had afflicted the Maxwells; such letters between a young husband and his wife are otherwise bewildering. Campbell, who may have been privy to Maxwell's confidence, offers little beyond these highly selective quotes.

Oddly enough, for the first fifteen years of his marriage, Maxwell seems to have written no poetry – humorous or other. We know little, then, of what may or may not have lain hidden away from prying eyes beneath the peaceful externals, the quiet day-by-day routines of the Maxwells' existence. After the Aberdeen years, the emotional, private domains are covered by a veil. Maxwell's intellectual life, though, was in rolling ferment. It was then, between the ages of twenty-nine and thirty-four, that he did much of his greatest work.

Maxwell's activities during the London years were varied and brilliant. Best appreciated by his coevals, because most easily understood, was his work on colour. For this he received in 1860 the Royal Society's Rumford medal. He continued his researches on the subject during the first year or two in London. Experimental facilities at the college were limited, and he did much of his observing at home. His optical experiments in fact aroused some curiosity amongst his Kensington neighbours. He used a long wooden box of his own design – his colour box, he called it – with the sun as a light source. He spent many hours bent over it, by an open upper-floor window of the house. Neighbours believed he was busy staring into a coffin and concluded that he was a very strange man – the prototypical mad professor, no doubt. In May 1861 Maxwell gave a lecture on his colour investigations at the Royal Institution, at which he displayed the first colour photograph. The principle was simple: take a black and white photograph through three filters – green, red and blue, then project and superpose the results through the same filters. Maxwell used a Scottish tartan ribbon with good results. It was subsequently pointed out that the collodion process he used should not have worked because it was not red-sensitive. But then it was shown that the process was sensitive to the ultraviolet passed by the filter. Maxwell had been very clever; he had also been lucky.

Much interesting experimental work was carried out in the attic at 8 Palace Gardens Terrace. Between 1863 and 1866 measurements made there verified some of the more remarkable results of the molecular theory of gases – notably Maxwell's 1859 prediction that viscosity – the fluidity, or rather the opposite thereof – is independent of density. Maxwell designed an apparatus to determine viscosity by measuring the damping of oscillations of disks suspended by a thin wire in a hermetically sealed vessel – which he described in detail in his 1866 Bakerian Lecture to the Royal Society. These experiments, more than anything, satisfied Maxwell of the correctness of his views on gases and encouraged him to pick up the threads of his Aberdeen work. This led to a celebrated paper – *On the Dynamical Theory of Gases* (1866) – the significance of which for modern science we shall examine later. Katherine was of great help in these experiments – assisting among other things in maintaining constant temperatures in the garret. From at least one point of view, then, it seems that Maxwell's marital life was progressing satisfactorily. One may usefully contrast it to Rumford's, an earlier experimenter: it is said that whilst this gentleman was conducting scientific measurements at home *his* wife poured boiling water on his favourite rose beds. But perhaps this had to do with the fact that Rumford was a notorious philanderer – which Maxwell most certainly was not.

The principal achievement of Maxwell's London years – his greatest masterpiece – was embodied in a series of articles on electromagnetic theory, articles in which the celebrated *Maxwell's Equations* first saw the light of day. Entitled *On Physical Lines of Force* (in four parts, beginning in 1861) and *A Dynamical Theory of the Electromagnetic Field* (1864 – published in 1865, in seven parts), they have been the subject of much scholarly and scientific analysis. Most of this is fairly technical and apt to leave the layperson with the feeling that an understanding of Maxwell's true greatness is reserved for the expert. Such an impression would be quite false. Technicalities are inessential ingredients of Maxwell's thinking. His electromagnetic theory can be appreciated by the non-scientist on a far more basic level – as a series of profound new insights into the foundations of our universe, as a real revolution in mankind's thinking.

It is maintained too often that the savouring of great scientific discoveries requires a degree of technical mastery of the subject matter. This is true only if one is intent upon admiring the fine craftsmanship that is often involved. But if the work be truly significant, the main lines of thought are always straightforward and reasonably accessible. One's wonderment at a remarkable breakthrough can be sharpened by delving into technicalities; the expression of genius requires a command of tools – it involves an important element of technique. But greatness in science is far more than craft or even virtuosity; it is, indeed, much rarer than either. The physicist's tools – his mathematical language, his experimental know-how – bear the same relationship to his thought as the brushwork of the artist bears to the whole painting. They are important. Yet the lover of art can extract the essence of a Rembrandt without understanding or even caring much about technique. The message is accessible to millions because it transcends its craft. In the same way Maxwell's significance in the history of scientific thought – of human thought – shines through the mere technicalities of his research. Maxwell himself was unusually adept at explaining in ordinary language the meaning of his ideas – an uncommon talent amongst scientists. Faraday, whose knowledge of mathematics was negligible, was perforce a master of this kind of exposition; but he pays tribute to this ability of Maxwell's in a letter written in 1857:

> There is one thing I would be glad to ask you. When a mathematician engaged in investigating physical actions and results has arrived at his conclusions, may they not be expressed in common language as fully, clearly, and definitely as in mathematical formulae? If so, would it not be a great boon to such as I to express them so? – translating them out of their hieroglyphics, that we might also work upon them by experiment. I think it must be so, because I have always found that you could convey to me a perfectly clear idea of your conclusions, which, though they may give me no full understandng of the steps of your process, give me the results neither above nor below the truth, and so clear in character that I can think and work from them. If this be possible, would it not be a good thing if mathematicians, working on these subjects, were to give us the results in this popular, useful, working state, as well as that which is their own and proper to them?

However, to appreciate Maxwell's greatest work, on whatever terms, it must be put in the context of the history of the sciences of electricity and magnetism. It is then seen for what it is: a turning point in man's view of the universe, a revolution in thinking having incalculable philosophical and technological repercussions. Once this is understood one must agree with Feynman's assessment and conclude with him that, if our race survives the current period of technological and social upheavals, Maxwell's discoveries may prove to have been the most important event in nineteenth-century history.

9

ELECTROMAGNETISM, LIGHT, AND MAXWELL

Consciousness of electrical phenomena is as old as consciousness itself. Lightning, stingrays, electric eels, static charges in dry climates – all were experienced by early man. More recent, yet still of prehistoric origin, is the awareness of magnetism – of the mysterious properties of the lodestone, the attractions and repulsions between fragments of magnetized ore. While the Chinese are said to have observed these long before our Christian era, the earliest *recorded* interest in such matters comes from the Greeks. Thales of Miletus is known to have studied the lodestone; Aristotle reports him as saying 'That the magnet has a soul because it moves the iron.' These early pre-Socratics were curious also about the electrical charge generated by rubbing amber. Yet it would take about two and a half thousand years before this kind of electricity was seen to be the same as that found in eels, stingrays or lightning. And it is barely a hundred years since the intimate relationship between electricity and magnetism – their *sameness* – has been understood. A difficult, tortuous, infinitely slow history of investigation extends from man's first iron-age confrontation with magnetism, from Thales to Faraday and Maxwell.

The Greeks, then, as well as the Chinese, had long been aware of magnetism. So had others: according to Hindu tradition Susruta, a Benares surgeon of the sixth century BC (the age of the Buddha), used magnets for surgical purposes. The first certain observation of the directional properties of a magnet in the Earth's field came a thousand years later in China, where in the fifth century AD Tsu Ch'ung-chih invented a 'South-pointing vehicle'. The earliest use of the magnetic compass for navigational purposes was probably by Muslim sailors plying between Canton and Sumatra towards the end of the eleventh century. In Europe the compass was mentioned towards the turn of the twelfth century by Alexander Neckam, abbot of Cirencester and suckling brother to Richard I. In the early thirteenth century, so Sarton assures us, a Muslim writer speaks of 'a sailor finding his way by means of a fish rubbed by a magnet' – surely one of the more exotic navigational uses of magnetism.

In the second half of the thirteenth century Peter the Stranger (Peregrinus), a Picard crusader and teacher of Roger Bacon – and, with him, the greatest physicist of medieval times – wrote a summary of magnetic knowledge then available. He describes a floating compass provided with a reference line and a circle divided into degrees, and experimental techniques for determining the poles of a lodestone, for magnetizing iron, etc. He is also on record as attempting to create a *perpetuum mobile* using magnets. In France Jean de Jaudun, in the early fourteenth century, wrote about magnets and the problem of action-at-a-distance. He assumed that between a magnet and a piece of iron attracted by it there exists a kind of medium which is gradually altered as the *species magnetica* is transmitted step by step – clearly anticipating our aether and field concepts. At some time during the Middle Ages, one cannot be sure when, navigators became conscious of the *declination* of the compass needle, i.e. of the fact that it deviates from true North; it is possible the Vikings already had this knowledge. By the time of Columbus it was well known.

In addition to deviating from true North, a freely suspended compass needle will also point downwards (*inclination* or dip): this was discovered during the Renaissance. Sir William Gilbert of Colchester (1540–1603), court physician to Queen Elizabeth and one of this period's most outstanding men of science – the first, according to some, to seriously practice the experimental method – carried out a series of studies on magnetism. His measurements of declination and dip led him to see the Earth itself as a great magnet, its poles offset slightly from the geographic ones. Like Thales he thought magnets to possess a strange spiritual quality; the soul of the Earth, he said, was its magnetic field. Gilbert also studied electrical effects; it was he who, after observing the charge, developed by rubbing various bodies such as amber, chose the Greek root (Greek for amber is *ēlektron*) and coined the term electricity.

The variation of the declination through the centuries was established early in the seventeenth century. Or at least it then became a matter of record – the history of these early observations is obscure, and one cannot exclude the possibility of ancient navigators having discovered these effects, perhaps much earlier.

In the eighteenth century knowledge of electricity and magnetism acquired a firm scientific base. It became recognized, for instance, that there were two kinds of electrical charge: rubbing glass with silk gave a vitreous electricity which would neutralize the resinous charge obtained by rubbing amber with fur. This led to two theories of electricity. One subscribed to the existence of two distinct, imponderable fluids, a positive and a negative, corresponding to two kinds of charge. The rival theory said there was only one such fluid, any deficiency of which created an apparent charge of the opposite kind. Essential facts were established: like charges repel and opposite charges attract; there are bodies through which electricity flows easily (conductors) and others which oppose the flow (insulators). Benjamin Franklin (1706–90) – he who, according to his epitaph, 'snatched lightning from the heavens and sceptres from kings' – showed that lightning is electricity, that charge is conserved and that there is action-at-a-distance between charges. And through a brilliant piece of deductive reasoning Joseph Priestley (1733–1804) was the first to infer that this takes place according to a law similar to Newtonian gravitation – with a force proportional to the inverse distance squared. Cavendish (1731–1810) also reached this conclusion around 1774, although his work remained largely unknown until its editing a century later by Maxwell. In the meantime John Mitchell (1724–93) at Cambridge had in 1750 published a memoir on magnets, showing how the force between magnetic poles followed the same rule. This basic law of action-at-a-distance became generally accepted after Coulomb (1738–1810) in France verified it directly with a torsion balance (1785); it has since been known as Coulomb's law. But the credit must rightly belong to, or at least be shared by Mitchell, Priestley, and Cavendish.

In this way the lore of electricity and magnetism became science during the second half of the eighteenth century. Conservation of charge and Coulomb's law allowed the mathematicians to erect a theoretical structure to interact systematically with experimental work – in the manner in which astronomy and mathematics had done since Newton. In France, Poisson (1781–1840) developed the theory of forces between electrified or magnetized bodies to a high degree of refinement and George Green (1793–1841) established the enormously useful concept of potential (a quantity whose rate of change is the force acting upon a small charge). By the time Maxwell began his researches the study of static charges and magnetic poles – electrostatics and magnetostatics – had reached a high level of sophistication. It was a triumph of action-at-a-distance, Newtonian-style physics. As in the earlier evolution of mechanics, statics had developed first, and for good reason: it is simpler than dynamics. Nature, however, is not static. Charges or magnetic poles exert forces on each other and forces produce *motion*.

Important was the fact that electrical charge moves easily and rapidly through conductors. But until the turn of the century the only known method of storing electricity was the

Leyden jar – a kind of glass bottle with conducting coatings inside and out. One could store unpleasantly large charges this way, as demonstrated by several European monarchs who, as entertainment for their courts, organized the electrification of whole brigades of soldiers – perhaps one of history's more benign uses of the military. But such Leyden jar currents were dissipated in one quick discharge; the jars then had to be recharged: there was no convenient way of generating a steady current. Under these circumstances, the knowledge of currents and the dynamics of electricity could only progress slowly. All this changed dramatically at the end of the century.

The breakthrough, as is so often the case, was made serendipitously. Galvani (1737–98), professor of anatomy at Bologna, observed a strange thing. He had:

> Dissected and prepared a frog, and laid it on a table, on which, at some distance from the frog, was an electric machine. It happened by chance that one of my assistants touched the inner crural nerve of the frog with the point of a scalpel; whereupon at once the muscles of the limbs were violently convulsed.
>
> Another of those who used to help me in electrical experiments thought he had noticed that at this instant a spark was drawn from the conductor of the machine. I myself was at the time occupied with a totally different matter; but when he drew my attention to this, I greatly desired to try it for myself, and discover its hidden principle. So I, too, touched one or other of the crural nerves with the point of a scalpel, at the same time that one of those present drew a spark; and the same phenomenon was repeated exactly as before.

He went on to show more generally how these convulsions occurred whenever a connexion was made between the nerves and the muscles by a metallic circuit, preferably of more than one metal. Whereas he ascribed this to a kind of biological current, he had actually stumbled on the principle of the battery. A compatriot physicist – Alessandro Volta (1745–1827) – showed that what Galvani had actually done was to use biological tissue as a fluid layer between two metals. A continuous current, he ascertained, could be generated by putting a damp cloth or moist pasteboard between two plates – one of zinc and the other of copper. This *Volta cell*, the first battery, would henceforth provide physicists with a continuous source of electricity. It marked the beginning of the quantitative study of currents. This in turn opened the way to the synthesis of electricity and magnetism.

A relationship between electricity and magnetism had been suspected for some time. One of the first suggestions of this emanates from the experience of a Wakefield tradesman published in the *Philosophical Transactions* of 1735:

> Having put a great number of knives and forks in a large box, and having placed the box in the corner of a large room, there happen'd in July, 1731, a sudden storm of thunder, lightning, etc., by which the corner of the room was damaged, the Box split, and a good many knives and forks melted, the sheaths being untouched. The owner emptying the box upon a Counter where some Nails lay, the Persons who took up the knives, that lay upon the Nails, observed that the knives took up the Nails.

Efforts were subsequently made, notably by Benjamin Franklin, to demonstrate a relationship between electricity and magnetism. But the first unambiguous, repeatable result was obtained only in 1820, when the Dane Ørsted (1771–1851) found that a compass needle placed parallel to a current-carrying wire was deflected. This observation aroused immediate interest, notably amongst French physicists such as Biot, Savart and the great André Marie Ampère (1775–1836), who set about measuring and calculating the magnetic forces generated by electric currents. Ampère formulated a full theory of these and thereby laid the foundation of the modern view which sees magnetic forces as electrical phenomena: the magnetic properties of matter are due to the action of huge numbers of molecular and atomic magnets, in which submicroscopic electric currents are perpetually flowing in closed circuits, creating elementary magnetic fields. Maxwell speaks of Ampère's theory as 'one of the most brilliant achievements in science' and refers to its author as the 'Newton of Electricity'.

Yet even after Ampère's work the picture remained incomplete. If electric currents generate magnetic forces the converse, it seemed, should be true; on the grounds of symmetry, if nothing else, one expected the relationship to be two-way. Static electricity on a body, it was known, induced the appearances of an opposite charge on a neighbouring one: it seemed logical that moving charges in one conductor – i.e. a current – should, likewise, induce currents in another. In the late summer and autumn of 1831 Faraday did the famous experiments which showed just how this worked. Given two copper loops, a steady current in one produced *no* effect on the other. But a varying current gave a positive result: a change in the current of one loop created a *changing* magnetic field and *this* induced a current in the other loop. Ørsted had discovered that currents – moving charges – generate magnetic fields. Faraday showed that changing or moving magnetic fields generate currents. The circle was closed: electrical and magnetic phenomena were now linked, and the linkage had a curious symmetry – a kind of mutual embrace which was logically and aesthetically most satisfying.

At this time and in the years just after Faraday's discovery, no one, probably not even Faraday, understood how it presaged the eventual demise of what had been, heretofore, a securely mechanistic, Newtonian picture of the universe. Action-at-a-distance concepts, it seemed, were moving from strength to strength. In Germany in particular, Franz Neumann, Riemann, Kirchhoff, Weber – all famous names in the annals and textbooks of electromagnetism – were describing all electric and magnetic phenomena in these terms. Starting from a modified action-at-a-distance law for moving charges, Weber produced in 1846 what was probably the most brilliant formulation of this kind, explaining induction and most other known effects. In later years, while following his own, very different inspiration, Maxwell still treated Weber's views with great respect even though he saw serious objections to them.

By the 1850s and 1860s efforts were being made to visualize

mechanisms for the transmission of forces between charges and currents. Helmholtz, Kirchhoff, and others attempted to explain these in terms of pressures in a kind of imponderable fluid, imperceptible to our senses except through electrical or magnetic agencies. W. Thomson followed up Faraday's concepts with mathematical models, which were attempts to find analogues of electromagnetic forces in the behaviour of fluids and solids. We have seen, too, how in 1855 Maxwell had adapted this approach to his own interpretations of Faraday's views. Faraday and Maxwell together fathered the *field* concept. Faraday, probably the greatest experimental physicist the world has seen, came to it instinctively. One suspects that Maxwell, while he never actually said so, adopted this outlook for aesthetic reasons. For whatever reason, Faraday and Maxwell saw the lines of force, electric and magnetic, as real perturbations of the space surrounding charges, magnets and currents – as a *state* of an all-pervasive medium. For their predecessors and most of their contemporaries, who assumed that Coulomb's laws or modifications thereof were adequate to explain everything, the introduction of field ideas appeared unnecessary. Nevertheless, whatever their ultimate persuasion in this matter, physicists of the mid-century were beginning to see that space was more than a mere framework for matter to exist in; it had properties other than those of simple emptiness. Everything seemed to point to a kind of material substratum to the universe which transmitted force; according to Faraday and Maxwell, in fact, it was deformed by the forces of electricity and magnetism and stored their energies. This was the *electromagnetic aether*. There was no consensus on the nature of this medium. Yet liquid or solid, compressible or incompressible, massless or not, it – some agency, *something* – was required to explain the transmission of electrical and magnetic forces between two points.

Oddly enough another, hitherto unconnected, strand of natural philosophy had arrived at a similar conclusion: the theory of light had, independently, come to require the concept of an aether. The Greeks, who conceived most of our philosophical problems, are also the first on record to have wondered seriously about light. Pythagoras believed vision to be caused by particles emanating *from* the viewer. But according to Empedocles (fifth century BC) luminous bodies emitted emanations travelling with a definite speed. Aristotle quotes him in these terms;

> Empedocles says that light from the Sun arrives first in the intervening space before it comes to the eye, or reaches the Earth. This might plausibly seem to be the case. For whatever is moved (in space), is moved from one place to another; hence, there must be a corresponding interval of time also in which it is moved from the one place to the other. But any given time is divisible into parts; so that we should assume a time when the sun's ray was not yet seen, but was still travelling in the middle distance.

Hero of Alexandria (first century AD) appears to have demonstrated the basic law of reflection – the equality of angles of incidence and reflection. Insight into the physics of light progressed little in the Middle Ages, although practical optics advanced: Roger Bacon (1220–92) made many experiments with mirrors and lenses, and may even have anticipated the telescope. But one has to wait till the seventeenth century to see the nature of light being seriously debated.

Descartes (1596–1650) viewed the universe in mechanistic terms, as a plenum of matter imperceptible to the senses but capable of transmitting force and light. It was a complicated picture involving several types of universal matter, stirred by vortices and containing large numbers of minute globules. Light was transmitted between the latter as pressure, and colour was determined by their rates of spin. By a peculiarly inexact argument involving small particles of matter Descartes deduced the law of angles for the *refraction*, i.e. the bending of light rays as they pass from one medium into another. If one is to believe Huygens, Descartes actually lifted this law from an unpublished manuscript of the Dutchman Willebrod Snell.

The French have named this famous law after Descartes; the rest of the world calls it Snell's law.

Robert Hooke (1635–1703) believed light to be a vibratory displacement of a medium, through which it propagated at finite speed with associated motions which were 'exceeding small'. Newton (1642–1727), who quarrelled with Hooke over this and other things, was of the opinion that a kind of elastic medium or aether permeates all space and transmits vibrations as air propagates sound. However, these vibrations did not themselves constitute light, which he suggested might be best understood in corpuscular terms, as a stream of particles which excited aether vibrations of various pitches corresponding to different colours. Shortly after Hooke's and Newton's theories had appeared in print, the Danish astronomer Ole Rømer (1644–1710) made the first measurement of the speed of light in 1675. This he based on an astute interpretation of the observed eclipse times of Jupiter's moons. These, it had been noticed, varied in systematic ways as the distance between Earth and Jupiter changed over the years. Rømer showed how this could be accounted for by assuming light to take less time to travel from Jupiter to Earth when the two were close than when they were far apart. A simple calculation yielded 320,000 km per second for the speed of light; the modern figure is close to 300,000 km per second.

Christiaan Huygens (1629–1695) was a staunch defender of the vibratory or wave theory of light. In his view a crucial argument in favour of the theory was the lack of interaction between intersecting beams of light. Since furthermore light could travel through a vacuum, Huygens deduced that the medium supporting these vibrations – the aether – penetrated everything, including the vacuum. He gave much thought also to a strange optical phenomenon exhibited by Iceland spar (calcite) and other crystals: objects appear double when seen through a properly cut section. Light entering a crystal was, in other words, split into two rays, which have been called the ordinary and the extraordinary rays. Their behaviour, Huygens showed, depended upon the orientation of the crystal. The next logical step – to deduce that light itself had definite directional properties – was not taken for a hundred years. Nevertheless Newton, in a critique of Huygens' views, came very close when he pointed out why, in view of this phenomenon of double refraction, light waves could not be analogous to simple waves of compression like sound, but had to have what he called *sides*.

While during the next hundred years the physics of electricity and magnetism progressed swiftly, the theory of light remained quiescent. The field sprang spectacularly to life again in the hands of the great English scientist and polymath Thomas Young (1773–1829). A Quaker from Somerset and a man of outstanding gifts, Young knew eight languages by the age of fourteen, became a physician in 1799, was elected to the Royal Society at the age of twenty-one, and was professor of physics at the Royal Institution by 1801. He made first-rate contributions to physiology, to the theory of colour, to the decipherement of Egyptian hieroglyphics, and to physics. His most magnificent work was in the field of light; he is, with the Frenchman Fresnel, the father of modern optics. One of his earliest contributions, supportive of the wave theory, was the discovery of light interference in 1801. This process, previously seen and understood in the more concrete case of water waves, occurs when two trains of periodic waves travelling in different directions encounter each other. If they are of the same magnitude, an obvious thing happens; where the downward displacement of the surface due to one wave train meets an equal upward displacement of the other, the two motions cancel and the surface, at this point, remains undisturbed. This is an example of destructive interference. In places where the motions are in the same direction they add and reinforce each other, troughs are deepened, crests heightened: this is constructive interference. An optical phenomenon which had long puzzled physicists was the appearance of irridescent colours in thin films – e.g. oil on water – and of multicoloured rings in a lens in contact with a plate of glass (Newton's rings, which had so intrigued the youthful Maxwell). Young showed how these could be explained by the selective interference of various wavelengths of light. After he had published his results, he was immediately and virulently attacked in the *Edinburgh Review* by one Henry Brougham, an ambitious young lawyer with scientific pretensions. According to Whittaker, Brougham, who was to make a career in politics and became Lord Chancellor of England, actually succeeded with his attack in retarding for a while the progress of the wave theory – which nevertheless, thanks in large measure to Young's genius, was soon to emerge victorious.

Young decided next to look at another poorly understood problem: *diffraction* – the process by which wave energy travels around obstacles, as when light penetrates into regions of shadow or ocean waves get behind a breakwater. In optics it had been observed that dark and light bands or *fringes* formed in zones nominally in shadow. This, Young showed, could be explained by the interference of diffracted energy: another important blow had been struck for the wave theory. But defenders of the corpuscular view, such as Laplace, fought back strongly: the wave theory, they suggested, could not account for double refraction. Nor could it explain a phenomenon discovered by the French engineer Malus who showed that light reflected from a plane surface may, at certain angles of incidence, acquire properties similar to those observed for rays in crystals. Wishing to clinch the matter, the French Academy, which strongly favoured the corpuscular theory, proposed diffraction as the subject for the Academy's prize dissertation for 1818.

In response to this another engineer, Augustin Fresnel (1788–1827), submitted a memoir which contained the first complete explanation of diffraction. An obstacle takes a piece out of a travelling wavefront: one may think of an island or a rock blocking the path of a train of ocean waves. After passing the obstacle, one might expect, naively, the wave front to have

118

a kind of permanent hole in it – the shadow of the obstacle. What is observed in fact is that, as the wave travels away from the obstacle, the gap begins to fill – until at sufficient distance, all memory of the rock or island seemingly obliterated, the wave trains resume their course. This phenomenon is fundamental and typical of *all* forms of waves – sound, ocean waves, light. Fresnel proposed that the edges of the gap in the wavefront radiate secondary waves which, among other things, tend to fill it in. In his dissertation Fresnel offered calculations on the effects of strips and slits in a screen, backing these with detailed experimental results. Yet the members of the Academy commission, such as Laplace, Poisson and Biot, were doubtful. The story of how Fresnel actually convinced them is famous in the annals of science. Poisson noticed that, for a symmetrical obstacle like a circular disk, Fresnel's theory predicted a bright spot in the centre of the shadow, because all secondary waves interfere constructively at this point – which, he offered, was absurd and should be tested experimentally. This was promptly done, the bright spot was seen where it had to be, and Fresnel's theory dramatically vindicated. This singular victory for the wave theory of light was, in a sense, final. Henceforth it flourished – in the hands of Young and Fresnel at first, then with the co-operation of other great names of science.

In the minds of Fresnel, Young and a fellow-Scotsman of Maxwell's, David Brewster (1781–1868), the phenomena of double refraction led to the realization that light waves were in a real sense *transverse*. Vibrations of a taut string give a simple example of motion transverse to the direction of travel of a wave (travelling disturbance). Analogous is the case of so-called shear waves in a solid when the molecules of the body move transversely i.e. at right angles to the direction of travel. Just so *something* had to be vibrating transversely to the direction of the light ray. Contemporary mathematical work on elasticity showed how, among other things, two kinds of waves could propagate through the body of a solid: waves of compression, akin to ordinary sound, and waves of shear. Light, then, behaved analogously to shear waves in solids. The best analogy was proposed by James MacCullagh (1809–47), of University College Dublin, who used an incompressible solid – i.e. one which could transmit shear waves but not waves of compression.

By 1850 it was not only accepted that light consisted of waves, but also that these had to be transverse and were, in some sense, analogous to shear waves in solids. Of course if light were a form of wave motion, there had to be a medium – an aether – to carry it: this much had been obvious since the time of Huygens and Newton. It now looked as if this aether had to have properties similar to those of a solid. This raised many questions. The aether's presence, it seemed, should be detectable. Was it stationary? Did the Earth move through it? Or did it drag some along in its motion through the solar system and the stars? The Earth *appeared* to travel through – or with – this medium with great ease, without resistance or trace of an 'aether wind'. This luminiferous aether, in other words, was awkward. For that matter, what was its relationship to the electromagnetic aether? Were they distinct or one and the same? This last question was to be resolved by Maxwell with his theory of electromagnetism.

Maxwell's first paper on the subject, *On Faraday's Lines of Force*, appeared in 1855. A preliminary to his greatest work it was, in its author's modest estimation, no more than a systematic effort of collation, simplification and analogy, to allow the mind 'a clear physical conception, without being committed to any theory founded on the physical science from which that conception is borrowed . . .' The conception Maxwell borrowed, it will be remembered, was one of a massless, incompressible fluid – surrounding it with frequent warnings against taking the analogy literally. This paper was, largely, a kind of analogical and mathematical development of Faraday's results, in which Maxwell established mathematical modes of description he was to need in later developments. Thus he gave mathematical form to Faraday's somewhat mysterious electrotonic state – a quantity soon to be known as the vector potential, and for which Maxwell admits he can find no physical interpretation for, says he, 'it involves no physical theory, it is only a kind of artificial notation'. Maxwell makes only slight claims for this, his first profound piece of work, stressing how he wishes 'to avoid the dangers arising from a premature theory professing to explain the cause of the phenomena'. He is right, of course, in asserting that it does not offer a theory, yet he is being unduly modest – this paper is much more than the introduction of a new notation or a mathematical reformulation of Faraday's ideas. It is a definite step in the direction of a theory – one which furthermore shows an uncanny sureness in its choice of essentials. Most importantly, in it Maxwell adumbrates the ultimate course he will follow: the systematic development of the field point of view.

For Maxwell's theory itself we have to wait six years, until the famous *On Physical Lines of Force* appeared in four parts in the *Philosophical Magazine* in 1861/62. Here Maxwell first approaches the subject through a model, a fluid stirred by a great number of vortices – adjacent vortices, all revolving in the same direction. He shows how the forces of magnetism, at least, can be modelled by the pressure exerted by the motions of the vortices, the axes of which represent the magnetic field lines. But then Maxwell asks himself why the vortices in this model should be arranged the way they are, i.e. 'according to the known laws of lines of force about magnets and currents' and adds: 'we are now having to inquire into the physical connection of these vortices with currents, while we are still in doubt as to the nature of electricity . . .' He proceeds to tie the problem neatly to the obvious impossibility of conceiving wheel-like motions of perfect vortices in contact revolving in the same sense. Any youthful meccano devotee knows that gears or wheels in contact revolve in opposite directions. To have them turn in the same sense one must interpose an idle wheel. And so Maxwell assumes layers of small particles between his vortices, in a kind of rolling contact to act as idle wheels. A remarkable thing happens then: examining the motion of these particles, Maxwell recovers the correct mathematical relationships between currents and magnetic fields. An electric current, he concludes, is 'represented by the transference of moveable particles interposed between neighbouring vortices', and:

> It appears therefore that the phenomena of induced currents are part of the process of communicating the rotatory velocity of the vortices from one part of the field to another.

Maxwell demonstrates the compatibility of his model with most of the phenomena of electromagnetism – which can be identified with a variety of pressures, forces and motions in the hypothetical fluid. Nevertheless, he cautions:

> The conception of a particle having its motion connected with that of a vortex by perfect rolling contact may appear somewhat awkward. I do not bring it forth as a mode of connexion existing in nature, or even as that which I would willingly assent to as an electrical hypothesis. It is, however, a mode of connexion which is mechanically conceivable, and is easily investigated, and it serves to bring out the actual mechanical connexions between the known electrical phenomena; so that I venture to say that anyone who understands the provisional and temporary nature of this hypothesis, will find himself rather helped than hindered by it in his search after the true interpretation of the phenomena.

Maxwell, of course, believes in an aether – something which is stressed and set in motion, something to act as the seat of electromagnetic fields. But whatever its nature, this aether only behaves *analogously* to his model. The system of vortices and idle wheels is not a true picture – it merely has analogical value, as a kind of crutch for one's thinking. It shows how motion may be transmitted in ways reminiscent of the induction laws of electricity and magnetism: magnetic fields correspond to rotations, i.e. to spinning vortices, electric currents are represented by the motion of idle wheel particles, and so forth.

In part III of this long paper Maxwell addresses himself to the problem of how the rotations of the vortices – he now calls them cells – are actually transmitted through space. He then springs something new on the reader – something which has clearly been in the back of his mind all along:

> But it is necessary to suppose, in order to account for the transmission of rotation from the exterior to the interior parts of each cell, that the substance in the cells possesses elasticity of figure, similar in kind, though different in degree, to that observed in solid bodies. The undulatory theory of light requires us to admit this kind of elasticity for the luminiferous medium, in order to account for transverse vibrations. We need not then be surprised if the magneto–electric medium possesses the same property.

Maxwell, in other words, has been guided from the start by the idea that the electromagnetic and luminiferous aethers are the same (an idea previously advanced, as speculation, by Faraday).

The quasi-elastic properties of electrical media which Maxwell draws upon are evidenced in their simplest form by the behaviour of insulators, or *dielectrics*. In these, charge cannot flow freely, as it does in conductors. Yet if an electric field is applied to such a body, a small net displacement of charges does take place. Furthermore, this displacement is proportional to the electric field – the value of the constant of proportionality was available to Maxwell from experiments. Laws of this sort are typical of elastic effects – one needs only recall the behaviour of a spring, which is extended in direct ratio to the size of the force being applied (Hooke's *ut tensio sic vis*). It was logical for Maxwell to infer that the existence of electric displacements required the introduction of elastic effects into his model. This electric displacement is a limited excursion of charge – a net displacement thereof in an electric field. If the field is not steady, the displacement itself varies and constitutes a local motion of charge or current: the *displacement current*. The introduction of elasticity into Maxwell's model is thus equivalent to adding a displacement current to the flow of charge. The truly remarkable thing is that while Maxwell first applies this reasoning to bona fide dielectrics like air or glass, he ends up by using it also implicitly in empty space. This step is crucial to the whole theoretical edifice erected by Maxwell. Yet it has no logical justification. It is simply a splendid, anarchic inspiration – a stroke of genius. A consequence of this is that the aether has dielectric properties; this is what makes it analogous to a solid. The theory now predicts the existence of waves. These travel with the speed of light and consist of undulating magnetic and electric fields transverse to their direction of propagation. Says Maxwell, his triumph recorded for posterity in italics:

> *Light consists in the transverse undulations of the same medium which is the cause of electric and magnetic phenomena.*

Light, in other words, is an electromagnetic phenomenon and the luminiferous and electromagnetic aethers are one and the same.

The modern reader, contemplating Maxwell's baroque model of vortices and idle wheels, may be forgiven a twinge of doubt. It *is* bizarre – a kind of freak of the engineering imagination. But one must keep firmly in mind that Maxwell did not take his model literally. As he so often made it plain, he was an analogical thinker. Besides, the thought habits of his era demanded some sort of mechanism, however outlandish – everyone was offering up aether models; it was, one might say, the accepted language of the day. And in that mechanistically minded age, some took their models very seriously. Maxwell's friend, the great W. Thomson – Lord Kelvin – kept looking for improved aether mechanisms until the very end of his life.

Maxwell soon discarded his strange model. In his next paper, *The Dynamical Theory of the Electromagnetic Field*, the complicated structure of elastic vortices and idle wheels has disappeared, leaving only the essential mathematical theory. One commentator has likened this to Alice's Cheshire cat: the cat vanishes, but the grin remains. This work is Maxwell's crowning masterpiece:

> The theory I propose may . . . be called a theory of the *Electromagnetic Field* because it has to do with the space in the neighbourhood of the electric or magnetic bodies, and it may be called a *Dynamical* Theory, because it assumes that in that space there is matter in motion, by which the observed electromagnetic phenomena are produced.

The storage of electromagnetic energy in the field is then discussed in terms which no longer require his aether model. After writing down his final relations for the electromagnetic field (Maxwell's equations), he puts it this way:

> I have on a former occasion attempted to describe a particular kind of motion and a particular kind of strain, so arranged as to account for the phenomena. In the present paper I avoid any hypothesis of this kind; and in using such words as electric momentum and electric elasticity in reference to the known phenomena of the induction of currents and the polarization of dielectrics, I wish merely to direct the mind of the reader to mechanical phenomena which will assist him in understanding the electrical ones. All such phrases in the present paper are to be considered as illustrative, not explanatory.
>
> In speaking of the Energy of the field, however, I wish to be understood literally. All energy is the same as mechanical energy, whether it exists in the form of motion or in that of elasticity, or in any other form. The energy in electromagnetic phenomena is mechanical energy. The only question is, Where does it reside? On the old theories it resides in the electrified bodies, conducting circuits and magnets, in the form of an unknown quality called potential energy, or the power of producing certain effects at a distance. On our theory it resides in the electromagnetic field, in the space surrounding the electrified and magnetic bodies, as well as in those bodies themselves, and is in two different forms, which may be described without hypothesis as magnetic polarization and electric polarization, or, according to a very probable hypothesis, as the motion and strain of one and the same medium.

In part VI of this paper Maxwell offers the full, formal electromagnetic theory of light, showing the reader, in a few neat and simple lines, how it follows from his general equations for the field. This, in many ways, is the most beautiful and pleasing section – to which, no doubt, he is referring in an 1865 letter to Charles Cay when he says: 'I have also a paper afloat, with an electromagnetic theory of light, which, till I am convinced of the contrary, I hold to be great guns.' In this treatment, all observed properties of light – in solids, crystals, empty space – follow without further ado directly from the mathematics. No use of models is required. And the speed of light – as already shown in 1862 – also agrees with the predictions of the theory. It was indeed great guns.

For us, with our hundred or so years of perspective, these two papers – Maxwell's theory of electromagnetism – are a turning point in the history of science. The theory is, first of all, a synthesis – one of the greatest in the history of science. It unifies two kinds of force – the electric and the magnetic – under one: the electromagnetic field. This unification was the direct, logical consequence of Faraday's experimental work; it had been begun by others – Ampère, Weber, W. Thomson. But Maxwell crystallized this, the first of the modern unified field theories and gave it the mathematical form which remains immortal under the name of *Maxwell's equations* – a system of relationships between changing electric and magnetic fields – a whole universe of electromagnetic phenomena, miraculously contained in a few lines of elegant mathematics. These equations are, for the physicist, a vision of outstanding beauty – they led the great Boltzmann to quote Goethe: 'was it God who wrote these lines . . .' To the modern student, who has the added advantage of a compact modern notation, these relations seem astonishingly simple. Yet they are the culmination of centuries and millenia of painstaking research and careful thought. It is the privilege of genius to render simple that which once appeared difficult and complex.

Secondly, Maxwell's formulation of electromagnetism has had incalculable effects upon our civilization. Thus a logical sequel to understanding the nature of light was the prediction of similar forms of electromagnetic radiation at other wavelengths – of which radio, radar and television are prime examples. It is strange that Maxwell himself never tried to verify these obvious predictions of the theory, even though they must have been clear to him by the early 1860s. Direct experimental proof of the generation and transmission of such waves through space was obtained by Heinrich Hertz only in 1888. Then in 1896 Marconi obtained the first patent on 'wireless telegraphy' and radio was born. Practical radar and television followed in the 1920s and 1930s. There is hardly an area of modern technology and physics in which Maxwell's theory has not contributed something of importance – from electrical power generation and transmission to communication systems or the monster accelerators of modern particle physics. The scientific, practical, and engineering consequences of Maxwell's equations have been seminal, all-pervasive and quite impossible to list.

Maxwell's theory, however, was more than a synthesis or a source of future technologies. It involved a radical change in our conception of reality, a fundamental shift in point of view – it was what Thomas Kuhn has called a *scientific revolution*. Science, according to Kuhn, progresses discontinuously. During certain periods, a set theory is taken for granted: a given *paradigm* prevails (in physics, for instance, the Enlightenment and the first half of the nineteenth century was such a period, a time in which Newtonian mechanics reigned supreme). A great deal of good and even first-rate science is done in such times – this is what Kuhn calls 'normal science'. There is steady progress – some of it is consolidation, upholding the given wisdoms; some of it may undermine existing paradigms, raising awkward questions (the search for mechanical models of the luminiferous aether, for example, led to serious problems). Philosophical or other basic commitments, however, are not changed. Then an open, original mind, someone with less prior prejudice, arrives on the scene – a small boy in the crowd shouts 'The emperor has no clothes!' Suddenly, the point of view shifts; nothing henceforth looks the same. A *change in gestalt* has taken place.

Before Maxwell the world of physics was Newtonian. Except for Faraday, no one had much doubted that electricity and magnetism would be understood in terms of particles exerting forces upon each other, through what Koestler once called a grappling of ghostly fingers – an action-at-a-distance requiring no further elaboration. This approach, after all, had been eminently successful; it had coped well with gravity, astronomy and mechanics and normal research had become dedicated to the exploration of this paradigm. After Maxwell's great papers all this began to change. Increasingly, electricity and magnetism would be seen in terms of space-filling fields, fully and accurately defined by Maxwell's equations. Newtonian mechanics could not describe the behaviour of these fields; action-at-a-distance did not lead to a theory of light. These phenomena *transcended mechanics*. This change in viewpoint implied, as Kuhn puts it, 'a change in the rules governing the prior practice of normal science' and, of course, reflected upon the work of Maxwell's predecessors and of many of his contemporaries. As such it was not quickly or universally accepted. Even W. Thomson, whose insights had so encouraged and spurred Maxwell in his early work, referred in 1888 to Maxwell's theory as 'a curious and ingenious, but not wholly tenable hypothesis'. In 1904, shortly before his death, Thomson still maintained that 'the so-called electromagnetic theory of light has not helped us hitherto'. Scientific revolutions are not so different from their social counterparts; the proverbial reluctance of community elders to accept radical change is the same. A famous physicist once said that for a new theory to be accepted one must wait for its opponents to die. Perhaps so. Yet in a historical perspective, when seen against a backdrop of centuries or millenia, a generation is not a long time. The shift in gestalt is, in these terms, sudden enough.

Viewed with suspicion by Maxwell's contemporaries, the field paradigm became, in our century, the standard approach to many fundamental problems. Einstein used Maxwell's field equations as the basis for his Special Theory of Relativity. His

General Theory was a pure *field* theory of gravitation – without which modern cosmology, cosmogony, and astrophysics are inconceivable. In particle physics a multiplicity of fields are now used to characterize the subatomic world. These are *abstract* fields, describing forces and energies of which our senses have no experience. Maxwell's theory was a critical step towards this kind of increased abstraction. In his willingness to wrench himself from the concrete Maxwell was again far ahead of his colleagues. Unlike them, he never took models of the aether seriously, preferring to use them as mere analogies – as a kind of scaffolding which could later be discarded. He accepted the *existence* of an aether, but was entirely sceptical of models – as when, in discussing his vortices and idle wheels, be cautions of 'the provisional and temporary nature of this hypothesis', or, in talking of aether stresses and momenta, he warns that: 'All such phrases in the present paper are to be considered as illustrative, not as explanatory.'

Maxwell's scepticism foreshadows modern thinking on space, time and matter – which in effect says that, since the substructure of the world is impenetrable to our senses, it is unreasonable to expect it to behave in ways transparent to our normal intuitions. What the world regards as 'common sense' is but sense reared on everyday experience. Understandably it conforms in most ways to Newtonian physics, which had tackled only the most immediate aspects of the world, i.e. those accessible to our senses. In digging deeper, as in trying to explain electricity and magnetism, this common sense becomes a dubious guide. One then finds oneself limited to mathematics as a kind of ultimate structure – an abstract sort of understanding which nineteenth century natural philosophers found uncongenial. For these were mechanical-minded men and women, living in a mechanical age, and they looked for mechanical explanations. Maxwell himself couched much of his research and expository work on electromagnetism in such terms – but he was never satisfied with these, emphasizing always their purely *analogical* nature. In his theory of electromagnetism Maxwell was the first to concede implicitly that the fundamental realities of our world may be beyond the ken of our senses. He put into practice Kant's admonition that, whereas 'Hitherto it has been assumed that all our knowledge must conform to objects' we should see what happens 'if we suppose that objects must conform to our knowledge'. His willingness to do this he owed partly to his metaphysical bent, partly to the training he had received in Edinburgh under Hamilton. In some measure, too, it was a reflection of his genius – a genius compounded of an extraordinary physical insight, a seemingly endless capacity for work and a rare level of philosophical awareness.

10

GLENLAIR

Maxwell's social and private life in London between 1860 and 1865 seems to have been quiet and uneventful. Intellectually it was an immensely creative period, a time of research, of revolutionary insights and of inspired writing – years which saw the final making of his theory of electromagnetism. Happy and satisfying years in most ways; yet Maxwell's roots – and Katherine's – were in Scotland.

The contrast between London and Galloway was, and still is, extravagant. The city's monumental buildings, its shops and busy traffic – in Victorian times the world's greatest centre of commerce and power – a place of prodigious activity, home of Faraday, of the Royal Society and the Royal Institution, must have been in many ways exhilarating for Maxwell. It was also the London of Dickens, a restless place of sprawling slums, poverty, filth, hurrying street life and implacable fogs. The Maxwells were largely insulated from the hustle of city life, comfortable and warm in their Kensington home. Nevertheless it was for them always a pleasure to take the train north, to return via Carlisle, Dumfries and Dalbeattie to Glenlair, to the pure air and peaceful remoteness of the Scottish countryside.

In the early 1860s the house at Glenlair remained as it had been designed by Maxwell's father – an unusual double structure, like a pair of two-storeyed slate-roofed farmhouses twinned broadside, with four south-facing windows and a small gabled entrance hall jutting out of the east wall. A roomy enough building but, as Scottish laird's houses go, a modest one. The property covered some six thousand acres. At its northern edge rose Mochrum Fell – a thousand feet of rock, heather and bracken, and a pleasant summer afternoon's scramble. From its top one has an unobstructed view of the high Rhinns of Kells and all the hills of Galloway and Dumfriesshire – long running ridges of granite and crumbling slate, a landscape of changing shadows and shifting colour. From high ground on the estate, one sees on clear days, far across the Solway Firth to the south, the tender blue ridges of the English peaks. The house nestles in a valley, bounded to the east by the steep, rocky pastures of Bardarroch Hill and to the west by a broad sweep of hills and rolling fields, crossed by a carriage road Maxwell took often, on foot or on horseback, to go to Parton. On the estate was a scatter of farms – his tenants. Most, like Hillside, Blackhills or Nether Corsock still thrive today, raising sheep, cattle and the occasional crop of barley. This was the country his father had loved, the country of Maxwell's golden childhood years, the home to which he would always return.

In January 1865 Maxwell tendered his resignation to King's College. His love of Glenlair and his desire to spend more time there must have been important factors. He wished also to put into effect his father's plans for enlarging the house and in this he was very likely encouraged by his wife. The Maxwells continued to spend parts of the winter at Palace Gardens Terrace and after 1868 at another London address. And, never one to shirk what he saw as duty, he continued during the winter of 1866 his evening courses for working men. Another important motive for his resignation was that it freed him from teaching. Henceforth he could give more time to research and writing. As he put it a year or so later to C. B. Tayler: 'I have now my time fully occupied with experiments and speculations of a physical kind, which I could not undertake as long as I had public duties.'

Apart from the demands lecturing had made upon his time, he had not enjoyed the process itself. The London students were often rowdy, and he was neither a good teacher nor an effective disciplinarian. There has even been a long-standing legend – originating from the official King's College 1929 centenary history, no less – that Maxwell was, for this reason, asked to resign. But Professor Domb has shown rather covincingly that the original source of this information is flawed, and the story best buried.

And so in the spring of 1865 Maxwell returned to Glenlair, to his green braes and heather-covered ridges. Towards the end of the summer he was very ill. Whilst riding an unfamiliar horse he scraped his head on a tree branch; the wound became infected and he contracted erysipelas – a streptococcal disease often fatal in the days before modern drugs. Once again Katherine nursed him back to health. He wrote to Charles Cay in October:

> We have had very fine weather since you went away, but I was laid up for more than three weeks with erysipelas all over my head, and got very shaky on my pins. But I have been out for a fortnight, and riding regularly as of old, which is good for Katherine after the nursing, and I eat about double what any man in Galloway does, and I know nothing of it in half an hour; but my legs are absorbing the beef as fast as it is administered.

Otherwise the rustic life was all the Maxwells had hoped for – quiet, orderly and productive. Maxwell tended assiduously to his duties as laird, visiting tenants, caring for them in times of illness, occasionally reading the Scriptures at a sick man's bedside (in those cases, Campbell underlines, 'where such ministrations were welcome'). For the household, he conducted daily prayers. Sometimes Maxwell entertained – 'dining the valley in appropriate batches' as he once put it. With Katherine he did a lot of reading – Shakespeare, Milton,

Chaucer, Spenser. And, of course, there was churchgoing on Sundays – in Parton, across the western hills, and in Corsock where he became a kirk elder. He donated generously to the building of the Corsock church and the manse, which was completed in 1865. A contemporary describes him in these terms:

> A man of middle height, with frame strongly knit and a certain spring and elasticity in his gait; dressed for comfortable ease rather than elegance; a face expressive at once of sagacity and good humour, but overlaid with a deep shade of thoughtfulness; the features boldly but pleasingly marked; eyes dark and glowing; hair and beard perfectly black, and forming strong contrast to the pallor of his complexion.

In 1867, while their house was being enlarged, the Maxwells took a trip to Europe – the only time they left the British Isles. Going by boat to Italy, they were quarantined in Marseilles – where Maxwell spent some time ministering to his fellow-passengers acting, among other things, as water carrier for the party. During this voyage Maxwell, who had a gift for languages, became fluent in Italian and improved his French and German although, for some reason, he had difficulty with Dutch. In Florence, entirely by chance, they ran into the Campbells – to whom Maxwell, who had attended a concert in the Vatican, reported himself pleased with 'the Pope's band'.

Several deaths took place during this period of Maxwell's life. In 1869 his cousin Charles Cay died at the age of twenty-eight, probably of tuberculosis. A teacher of mathematics, a man of gentleness and warmth, he had long been a favourite relative. His death saddened Maxwell deeply; they had spent many a happy day together at Glenlair. Faraday's death, in August 1867, was not unexpected; he had long been ill. And in December 1868 Forbes died after a brief illness.

Maxwell cannot have been wholly satisfied with his life as a country gentleman, for in 1868 he applied for the principalship of St Andrews, vacated by Forbes' retirement earlier in the year. In this he was encouraged by Campbell, who would later

disingenuously deny involvement in the affair. Recently unearthed correspondence suggests that, once again, Maxwell's
professional course was a rocky one. He had no sense of smell
for problems of this sort; he was as innocent of academic
intrigue as he was of politics – or of those murky grounds
where the two meet. Early in November he visited St
Andrews. A few days later, having made up his mind, he
asked W. Thomson for a letter of recommendation. Then he
wrote to W. R. Grove, a London acquaintance and vice-
president of the Royal Institution, requesting assistance – a
good word, perhaps, to the Home Secretary or the Lord
Advocate, adding:

> I have paid so little attention to the political sympathies of scientific men
> that I do not know which of the scientific men I am acquainted with
> have the ear of the Government. If you can inform me, it would be of
> service to me.

Whether he received this help, or not, is unclear. But the job
went to another candidate – J. C. Shairp, professor of Latin
at the university. Shairp, though virtually unknown, was a
personal acquaintance of the Duke of Argyll, Chancellor of St
Andrews and a supporter of the Gladstone government which
came into power at that time.

These Glenlair years, 1865–71, were in no sense a period of
retirement or retreat. Throughout, Maxwell maintained a
phenomenal level of activity. The volume of his professional
correspondence grew so that he had to have a special letter box
sunk into the wall of the abutment of the bridge across the Urr.
Every day, in all weathers, he would walk the few hundred
yards to it to collect his bundles of letters, manuscripts, journals
and proofs. And as moderator or examiner at the Cambridge
tripos, he kept up his university ties.

These in fact were the years when Maxwell's output of
original work reached a peak – a display of scientific pyro-
technics covering geometry, optics, elasticity theory, electricity
and magnetism, thermodynamics and molecular theory. It is

difficult, without going into great technical detail, to do justice to Maxwell's brilliance during this time. Mention of a few outstanding results may give a pale reflection thereof.

In 1868 *On Governors* contains the first formulation of the theory of feedback – the foundation of what Norbert Wiener named cybernetics. In 1870 Maxwell's *On Hills and Dales* was the beginning of what is now a serious discipline, global analysis. In this paper Maxwell states the fundamental relationship on a topographic contour map between the number of peaks, passes, bottoms and ridges. Oxford's Professor Temple has dubbed this Noah's theorem: after all, Noah in his ark, watching the waters recede, would have been the first to see it demonstrated – a fantasy Maxwell would have enjoyed.

In 1870 Maxwell published also *The Theory of Heat*. In this book he offered his readers a playful and profound invention, a mythical being W. Thomson named *Maxwell's demon*. A creature small enough to see or sense individual molecules of gas, the demon is imagined in a gas-filled container which a barrier divides in two. In the barrier is a small valve – a sliding, frictionless, weightless trapdoor which can be operated without expending work. The demon proceeds to use this valve to sort molecules, for instance by letting through the fast ones from side A to side B and the slow ones from B *to* A. The end result of this activity is to collect fast molecules in B, leading to a hot gas, and slower ones in A (cool gas). And so, without doing work, the demon sorts out the molecules and produces a more highly ordered state, a temperature difference which can be used to produce work. The demon may thus, in principle, generate a *perpetuum mobile* – in direct contravention to the second law of thermodynamics. This creation – today we would call it a thought experiment – must have given Maxwell many a chuckle. To clarify its role he wrote to Tait:

Concerning Demons.
1. Who gave them this name? Thomson.
2. What were they by nature? Very small BUT lively beings incapable

of doing work but able to open and shut valves which move without friction or inertia.

3. What was their chief end? To show that the 2nd Law of Thermodynamics has only a statistical certainty.

But appealing to statistical validity was not the way out of the dilemma; as Maxwell suggested in another letter it actually cast doubt on the very validity of the second law. The demon was only properly exorcized some sixty years later when Szilard pointed out the intimate connexion between entropy and information. Information is negative entropy; one cannot obtain information about a system without increasing its entropy; the demon, by the very act of seeing or sensing the molecules, would be perturbing the system. In the 1940s it was further understood that it is actually impossible, as a matter of principle, for the demon to 'see' the molecules: the background thermal radiation, with which any enclosure is filled, rules it out. But for more that half a century, Maxwell's little demon made some very clever people think very hard indeed.

Between 1865 and 1871 Maxwell also wrote most of his *Treatise on Electricity and Magnetism*, plus sixteen scientific papers. Of the latter, the most brilliant and profound dealt with the molecular theory of gases. It is difficult to assign exact dates to a man's creative research: the moments of critical insight are often unknown, the gestation uncertain and sometimes not fully conscious. Maxwell's most important papers on molecular theory, published between 1866 and 1867, were undoubtedly conceived and begun in London. But they took final form during his Glenlair period. They represent the second major domain in Maxwell's work – the molecular or *atomistic* strand in his thought.

Atomism has ancient roots. Its earliest statement was by eastern philosophers, notably by Vardhamana (Mahavira) of the sixth century BC, an Indian contemporary of the Buddha and leader of the ancient Jain religion – a heretic separation of Brahmanism. Democritus of Abdera and his teacher Leucippus, in the fifth century BC, are usually credited with the first western formulation – but it is not known whether their ideas were original or inspired by eastern influences. In western thought there developed, after Aristotle, a split between atomists and Aristotelians. The notions of atom and vacuum were inseparable: a vacuum, said Democritus, was necessary for atoms to move in. But Aristotle ruled that a vacuum could not exist: neither then could there be atoms! Nevertheless, atomism was taken up and enlarged by Epicurus, who first introduced the idea of randomness as a *clinamen*, or a kind of atomic skewness or unruliness. In the first century BC atomism was popularized in Rome by Lucretius in his encyclopaedic poem *De Rerum Natura*. But to early Christians Lucretius' views on religion were anathema and this great work was ignored and buried. In the West, for a while, atomism was forgotten. Through the Middle Ages Aristotle was the final authority on all matters philosophical: Nature abhorred a vacuum, and that was the end of it. Like so much that was valuable in Greek thought, atomism survived in Islam and was reintroduced into European thought after the Dark Ages. Yet the Aristotelian view would only be finally laid to rest by the experimental creation of a vacuum in the seventeenth century by Otto von Guericke, and by Blaise Pascal whose barometric measurements on the Puy du Dome demonstrated that what held the fluid up inside a barometer was not the *horror vacui* but simple barometric pressure – the weight of the atmosphere.

Newton came to believe in a sort of static atomistic model of matter, in which molecules simply repelled each other without moving far. A more modern theory was proposed for gases by Daniel Bernouilli (1700–82) who showed that, if one imagined a gas to consist of huge numbers of molecules travelling in all directions, the sum total of their impacts on the wall of the container would create the observed pressure (1734). Pressure would thus increase in proportion to the compression of the gas – as well as to its rise in temperature (as had already been demonstrated experimentally by Boyle). Bernouilli's views acquired particular cogency early in the nineteenth century with the advent of the principle of energy conservation and the identification of heat with energy. Waterston (1845) and Joule (1848) estimated the velocities molecules should have in order to produce the observed pressures.

Following his work on Saturn's rings, which had led him to contemplate the behaviour of large numbers of particles, Maxwell read in 1859 a work by Clausius which illuminated the problem for him. He saw in particular that probability theory provided the key to the calculations. He then wrote, while still in Aberdeen, his first classic paper on the subject, *Illustrations of the Dynamical Theory of Gases*, which appeared in the *Philosophical Magazine* in January and July 1860. It marked the first time statistical methods had been used for formulating physical laws. It gave the probability for molecules to have velocities of motion within a given range of values – a famous relationship known as the Maxwell distribution. Maxwell also showed how to calculate some of the characteristics of the gas, such as its viscosity – which he predicted to be independent of the density. However, this classic and historic paper was flawed by several errors, which were quickly pointed out by Clausius. It is possible that Maxwell made the mistake, unusual for him, of rushing into print too fast. The first part of the paper was given at the British Association meeting in September 1859, not long after he had read Clausius' articles. Pleased with the elegance and simplicity of his method, he may have been eager to publish. In 1866 Maxwell's Bakerian lecture was largely an account of the measurements he had carried out in London, with Katherine's help, confirming among other things the predicted density independence of viscosity.

But his 1867 paper, *On the Dynamical Theory of Gases*, was a masterpiece. In it he explicitly acknowledges the errors of his 1860 work, graciously emphasizing Clausius' role in pointing them out:

> It is to Professor Clausius, of Zurich, that we owe the most complete dynamical theory of gases. His other researches on the general dynamical theory of heat are well known, and his memoir *On the Kind of Motion we*

Call Heat, are a complete exposition of the molecular theory adopted in this paper. After reading his investigation of the distance described by each molecule between successive collisions, I published some propositions on the motions and collisions of perfectly elastic spheres, and deduced several properties of gases, especially the law of equivalent volumes, and the nature of gaseous friction. I also gave a theory of diffusion of gases, which I now know to be erroneous, and there were several errors in my theory of conduction of heat in gases which M. Clausius has pointed out in an elaborate memoir on the subject.

Clausius, incidentally, had also used some faulty assumptions in *his* papers! The field, it will be understood, was in a state of turmoil.

On the Dynamical Theory of Gases accomplished some remarkable feats. In particular, it reconciled most of the observed properties of fluids with the theory – i.e. with the molecular models, and so put the whole subject on a secure theoretical footing. In it Maxwell introduced concepts and results which have ever since been part of the physicist's everyday repertory. A particularly simple and fundamental one is the idea of *relaxation*. Many phenomena in nature have a characteristic time scale; following inception, it takes a certain span of time for the process to run its course. Thus the motion of a weight attached to a spring can be damped and brought to an end by a viscous oil bath – as in a shock absorber: if displaced, the weight returns slowly to its original position. The time this takes is the *relaxation time* of the system. This, one might think, is obvious enough – trivial, almost, when stated in these terms. Yet much of physics is built up of such elementary concepts. The originality of great minds like Maxwell's often lies in their ability to be the first to recognize the importance of simple insights and knowing when to apply them. Maxwell introduced the concept of relaxation time in explaining the diffusion of stress in fluids. Unlike solids, fluids cannot, if sheared, maintain a stressed condition. The shear is dissipated within a characteristic time span – the relaxation time of the fluid. Maxwell related this to his molecular model: the viscosity of a fluid is due to the relaxation of such stresses by molecular collisions. Putting to use his gift for visualizing geometrical relationships in space and time, Maxwell calculated the rate of collisions of molecules for a variety of specific laws of repulsion; this allowed him to obtain formulas for the viscosity, heat conduction and other fundamental properties of a gas. It was a true molecular theory of matter, and a great achievement.

The details of *On the Dynamical Theory of Gases*, its impressive mathematical technique, its sharp insight are a theoretical physicist's delight. Ludwig Boltzmann, in Germany, whose contributions to the field of statistical physics are second to none, likened this work to a great symphonic poem and, generally speaking, went into paroxysms of delight over Maxwell's mastery. For some, this and one or two of Maxwell's later papers represent his most profound and mature scientific work. This may be so – although perhaps words such as mature and profound should be defined with care so that a common ground of meaning can be agreed upon. But no matter how one says it, this work is utterly remarkable and good grounds for professional ecstasy. Yet the consensus among modern physicists would be, I am sure, that Maxwell's theory of electromagnetism is still his greatest creation. The *Dynamical Theory of Gases* is a cornerstone of the nineteenth century view of matter. But it was not a scientific revolution – it did not lead to a shift in gestalt. Rather it was the deepening, the masterful development of a paradigm previously in use and already amplified by Clausius, Waterston, Joule and Bernouilli and originated by Democritus. One may say that, whereas Maxwell's theory of electromagnetism gives a true measure of his genius, his work on molecular theory is a monument to his profound physical insight.

11

RETURN TO CAMBRIDGE

The Old Cavendish, as it is now called, is not one of Cambridge's more beautiful buildings; yet it has a kind of Victorian, no-nonsense charm which pleases. The absence of neo-gothic frills, the square solidity and tall windows inspire confidence – this was once a functional edifice, built by pragmatic people for a practical purpose. James Clerk Maxwell, who helped design it, was its first director and worked here. So did Rayleigh, J. J. Thomson, Rutherford and many others. A good fraction of modern physics was born here.

In 1870 William Cavendish, the seventh Duke of Devonshire, member of the Royal Commission on Scientific Education and chancellor of the university, himself a mathematician of ability, donated funds to build a physical laboratory for Cambridge. In 1871 the university officially created a chair of experimental physics. It was offered first to W. Thomson who, comfortable in his Glasgow professorship, declined it. Helmholtz, the German physicist and physiologist, was also approached without success: he had just accepted a post in Berlin. In February 1871 Maxwell was contacted and there ensued a flurry of letters between him and the university. At first he was reluctant. As he put it to the Reverend Blore of Trinity College:

Though I feel much interest in the proposed Chair of Experimental Physics, I had no intention of applying for it when I got your letter, and I have none now, unless I come to see that I can do some good by it.

But various colleagues like Maxwell's old friend G. G. Stokes and J. W. Strutt (Lord Rayleigh – then, at the age of twenty-nine, a brilliant young Cambridge don) persuaded him to apply for the post. The offer came at a good time. The manuscript of the *Treatise on Electricity and Magnetism* was nearing completion and Maxwell was ready to undertake new work – in particular something which promised to give scope for his old love and interest in experiments. The attraction of having a whole laboratory at his disposal must have been very great.

To order his ideas and get a clear picture of what was needed Maxwell, thorough as ever, visited several laboratories including W. Thomson's in Glasgow. Upon his arrival in Cambridge he set to work enthusiastically, designing the building with the architect W. Fawcett, carrying out endless negotiations with instrument-makers, discussing matters with the vice-chancellor and the chancellor. He well knew the overweening, tyrannical importance of detail in experimental work, and he lavished great effort and attention on all particulars of the plans. He took infinite pains in selecting the best available equipment, checking and designing apparatus when necessary. He even spent generous amounts of his own money on instrumentation.

At the same time, he lectured. But his professorship was attached to the Cavendish and until this was built he had no place to call his own. As he put it in October 1872 to Campbell, with plaintive humour:

> Laboratory rising, I hear, but I have no place to erect my chair, but move about like a cuckoo, depositing my notions in the chemical lecture-room 1st term; in the Botanical in Lent, and in Comparative Anatomy in Easter.

Freshly appointed professors at British universities, by tradition, deliver an 'inaugural lecture'. This is usually a ceremonial affair at which the appointee is given licence to talk on some subject of his choice – so long as it bears a plausible relationship to his or her field of expertise. Maxwell began by giving the proceedings an unexpected twist. He announced his first lecture for undergraduates in terms which led people to think that this *was* the inaugural. Sir Horace Lamb (1849–1932), an applied mathematician of distinction and a Cambridge student at the time, recalls the result in these terms:

> The *dii majores* of the University, thinking that this was his first public appearance, attended in full force, out of compliment to the new Prof. and it was amusing to see the great mathematicians and philosophers of the place, such as Adams, Cayley, Stokes seated in the front row, while Maxwell, a perceptible twinkle in his eye, gravely expounded to them the relation between the Fahrenheit and Centigrade scales . . . It was rumoured Maxwell was not entirely innocent in this matter, and that his personal modesty, together with a certain propensity for mischief, had suggested this way of avoiding a more formal introduction to his Cambridge career.

This rekindles memories of the small boy who, on a winter evening in Glenlair, having blown out the candles, lay down across the doorway before the maid entered with the dinner tray. In his fortieth year, Maxwell's sense of fun was as irreverent as ever.

He atoned shortly thereafter with a superb inaugural entitled 'Introductory Lecture on Experimental Physics', though he still could not resist taking a gentle dig at the university in his opening sentence:

> The University of Cambridge, in accordance with that law of its evolution, by which, while maintaining the strictest continuity between the successive phases of its history, it adapts itself with more or less promptness to the requirements of the times, has lately instituted a course of Experimental Physics.

The lecture was a lucid statement of his views of science – stressing, as the occasion obviously demanded, the importance of correlating theory with experiment. Here Maxwell articulates with great clarity the effort needed for the practice of scientific thought:

> It is not till we attempt to bring the theoretical part of our training into contact with the practical that we begin to experience the full effect of what Faraday has called 'mental inertia' – not only the difficulty of recognizing, among the concrete objects before us, the abstract relation which we have learnt from books, but the distracting pain of wrenching the mind away from the symbols to the objects, and from the objects back to the symbols. This however is the price we have to pay for new ideas.
>
> But when we have overcome these difficulties, and successfully bridged the gulf between the abstract and the concrete, it is not a mere piece of knowledge that we have obtained: we have acquired the rudiment of a permanent mental endowment. When, by a repetition of efforts of this kind, we have more fully developed the scientific faculty, the exercise of this faculty in detecting scientific principles in nature, and in directing practice by theory, is no longer irksome, but becomes an unfailing source of enjoyment, to which we return so often, that at last even our careless thoughts begin to run in a scientific channel.

Maxwell is also concerned with the scientist's image:

> It is not so long ago since any man who devoted himself to geometry, or to any science requiring continued application, was looked upon as necessarily a misanthrope, who must have abandoned all human interests, and betaken himself to abstractions so far removed from all the world of life and action that he has become insensible alike to the attractions of pleasure and to the claims of duty.
>
> In the present day, men of science are not looked upon with the same awe or with the same suspicion. They are supposed to be in league with the material spirit of the age, and to form a kind of advanced Radical party among men of learning.

In many ways the nineteenth century was, compared to ours, a time of optimism. Science was indeed seen as a radical, enlightened enterprise. Maxwell, however, does not seem fully convinced. But his doubts stem more likely from religious and social conservatism, rather than from scepticism over the long term benefits of science and technology. He certainly rejects the distaste of the Romantics who, in the words of William Blake, saw the scientific mind as 'The Idiot Reasoner' who 'laughs at the man of Imagination' or, like Keats, lamented that

> . . . all charms fly
> At the mere touch of cold philosophy.

Well aware of this type of criticism, Maxwell defends science:

> The habit of recognizing principles amid the endless variety of their action can never degrade our sense of the sublimity of nature, or mar our enjoyment of its beauty. On the contrary, it tends to rescue our scientific ideas from that vague condition in which we too often leave them, buried among the other products of a lazy credulity, and to raise them into their proper position among the doctrines in which our faith is so assured, that we are ready at all times to act on them.

Nearing the end of his lecture, he offers his own brand of scientific romanticism:

> we gladly return to the company of those illustrious men who by aspiring to noble ends, whether intellectual or practical, have risen above the region of storms into a clearer atmosphere, where there is no misrepresentation of opinion, nor ambiguity of expression, but where one mind comes into closest contact with another at the point where both approach nearest to the truth.

This printed lecture, like all samples of his prose, makes it difficult to believe that Maxwell was not a good teacher. Yet this was undeniably so. According to Ambrose Fleming, a student at Cambridge in the late 1870s, Maxwell's lectures were poorly attended – pitifully so: when he first arrived at the university he was shocked to find Maxwell lecturing to a class of two or three, instead of the hundred or more attentive listeners he may have had in a Scottish or German university (Fleming could have been thinking, amongst other examples, of P. G. Tait whose courses in Edinburgh attracted numerous students). Maxwell's lectures were difficult to follow for all but the very best undergraduates. Not only was his elocution poor but, as Sir Horace Lamb has testified, he got himself into trouble at the blackboard. He wandered and had difficulty in seeing the obstacles experienced by lesser minds. As Tait put it in an 1880 *Nature* article:

> the rapidity of his thinking, which he could not control, was such as to destroy, except for the highest class of students, the value of his lectures. His books and his written addresses (always gone over twice in MS) are models of clear and precise exposition; but his *extempore* lectures exhibited in a manner most aggravating to the listener the extraordinary fertility of his imagination.

It is one thing to communicate ideas and concepts lucidly in writing; it is quite another to lecture undergraduates.

Yet because of his charm and his insight in guiding research students, Maxwell's directorship of the Cavendish was an outstanding success. In W. Thomson's words in 1882: 'There is, indeed, nothing short of a revival of Physical Science at Cambridge within the last fifteen years, and this is largely due to Maxwell's influence.' Among those who profited by their association with Maxwell at the Cavendish, as students or collaborators, were men like Fleming (who invented the vacuum-tube), Napier Shaw (the founder of British meteorology), J. W. Strutt – Lord Rayleigh – (the father of modern acoustics and of much else in modern physics).

Apart from teaching and overseeing research at the laboratory, Maxwell examined students, refereed papers for journals, wrote reviews and encyclopaedia articles and gave popular lectures. He also undertook to edit a collection of Henry Cavendish's unpublished papers dealing with experiments in electricity, many of which he carefully repeated and checked. As a result Cavendish's name is enshrined where it belongs – among the earliest masters of experimental electricity and the first, with Priestley, to have formulated 'Coulomb's Law' of force between charges in 1773.

This absorbed a lot of Maxwell's time – which, it has been said, might have been better spent on research. Yet during this period he also did much creative work. Maxwell's writings in the 1870s are scattered over many fields – thermodynamics, statistical mechanics, electromagnetism, capillarity, mechanics, optics. Three pieces of work stand out with particular vividness.

A Treatise on Electricity and Magnetism, the first publication of which by the Clarendon Press in 1873 is, after Newton's *Principia*, the most famous book in the history of physics. About four hundred thousand words long, crammed with references to contemporary and earlier research literature, its purpose was twofold: to give the world the first systematic account of Maxwell's electromagnetic theory while, at the same time, helping him order his own ideas on the subject. With characteristic modesty and fairness it begins by giving Faraday a large share of the credit:

> If by anything I have here written I may assist any student in understanding Faraday's modes of thought and expression, I shall regard it as the accomplishment of one of my principal aims – to communicate to others the same delight which I have found myself in reading Faraday's researches.

Starting from fundamentals the *Treatise* develops the field viewpoint which, says Maxwell, 'may in some parts appear less definite' than action-at-a-distance theory but 'corresponds more faithfully with our actual knowledge, both in what it affirms and in what it leaves undecided'.

Systematic, scholarly and profound, it is a paradoxical book – of which it is sometimes said that, despite its qualities, it could hardly be recommended as a textbook for students. It is composed in peculiar oracular style, as a sequence of numbered, declarative paragraphs – reminiscent of Wittgenstein's *Tractatus*, although perhaps less obscure. It consists of four parts: Electrostatics, Electrokinematics, Magnetism and Electromagnetism. For best results Maxwell recommends that these be read *concurrently*! In subsequent printings most of the errors have been weeded out; the original edition, however, contained a fair collection – Maxwell's lordly attitude towards inaccuracies in sign or numerical values was a source of considerable unhappiness to contemporaries and immediate successors who tried to apply his results. As Kirchhoff once remarked: 'He is a genius but one must check his calculations before one can accept them.' It was nevertheless a remarkable work, a labour of love which inspired many a physicist after Maxwell – not least of whom, at the turn of the century, would be the youthful Albert Einstein.

In this, Maxwell's *magnum opus* on electromagnetism, mention of his prior mechanical models of the aether occurs only once, when he refers to his 1861 paper:

> The attempt which I then made to imagine a working model . . . must be taken for no more than it really is, a demonstration that mechanism may be imagined capable of producing a connexion mechanically equivalent to the actual connexion of the parts of the electromagnetic field. The problem of determining the mechanism required to establish a given species of connexion between the motions of the parts of a system always admits of an infinite number of solutions.

His 1861 model, which he calls a theory of molecular vortices, is mentioned only as a sequel to some remarks by W. Thomson. Otherwise it plays no further role in Maxwell's theory. He did not of course discard the concept of an *aether*, even if he did not commit himself to a model thereof. In a later *Encyclopaedia Britannica* article entitled *Ether* he states:

> Whatever difficulties we may have in forming a consistent idea of the constitution of the aether, there can be no doubt that the interplanetary and interstellar spaces are not empty, but are occupied by a material substance or body, which is certainly the largest, and probably the most uniform body of which we have any knowledge.

Curiously, in the *Treatise* the word aether is mentioned only once. The book is in fact very modern in spirit. Included also are some new results – in particular, a calculation of the *radiation pressure* of light: Maxwell was the first to show that light waves falling on an object exert a force on it, tending to push it away. The force is small and difficult to observe, but can be measured.

The concept of radiation pressure is linked in an interesting way to other highly important endeavours of Maxwell's. In 1874 William Crookes had constructed a radiometer – an evacuated glass vessel inside which was a paddle wheel of lightweight vanes silvered on one face and blackened on the other. When a source of heat is put near it, it begins to spin. When first observed, this seemed to be a totally new effect. Between 1875 and 1877 hundreds of papers were written in scientific journals on the subject. It was eventually assumed that Maxwell's radiation pressure explained the motion of the paddle wheel. But it was soon understood that, when compared carefully to Maxwell's predictions, the effect was too large and in the wrong direction. Maxwell and Osborne Reynolds – an outstanding fluid dynamicist – concluded, more or less simul-taneously, that the secret lay in forces set up by temperature gradients in the remnants of the highly rarefied gas inside the vessel. Maxwell published his analysis in a landmark 1879 work: *On Stresses in Rarefied Gases Arising from Inequalities of Temperature*. He had experimented himself with the radiometer at the Cavendish, and this paper was a magnificent example of what he had described in his inaugural lecture as 'bridging the gulph between the abstract and the concrete' and acquiring thereby 'the rudiment of a permanent mental endowment'. The permanent endowment in this case was the theory of rarefied gases which he developed to account for the ob-servations – a whole new branch of physics without which we would today understand neither the upper atmosphere nor the fringes of space.

The intimate history of this study involved an unfortunate interplay of personalities – between Maxwell and his friends on one side and Osborne Reynolds on the other. It appears that in January 1879 Reynolds' article on the radiometer was sent to Maxwell for refereeing, that he made use of the ideas therein –

a fact acknowledged in his paper – and submitted a critical review. After an exchange of letters between the various participants Maxwell delivered himself in September of a scathing letter to Stokes:

> Of course I cannot profess to follow with minute attention the course of an acrobat (Reynolds) who drives 24 in hand, but as on more than one occasion he throws up the reins and starts a new team, it is probable that the results will be sufficiently flexible to adapt themselves to the facts, whatever the facts may be . . . I am afraid I have not answered your letter at all, except about O. R. being the discoverer of dimensional properties in gases. I have always felt inclined to give him leave to practice at his 'mean range' till he has qualified himself to go in among all comers for the R. S. meetings.

These comments reached Reynolds who understandably took umbrage; he long bore a grudge against Maxwell. Reynolds was in fact a first-rate man who contributed importantly to the physics of fluids and Maxwell's remarks were uncharacteristically lacking in generosity.

During these years at the Cavendish, Maxwell experienced a revival of his interest in the kinetic theory of gases. Not long before his paper on rarefied gases, he had published *On Boltzmann's Theorem on the Average Distribution of Energy in a System of Material Points*, in which he introduced a celebrated idea known as *the ergodic hypothesis*. This assumes that, given a very large number of molecules in a container and enough time, the molecules will ultimately have come to occupy every point in space and will have had all possible speeds within this container. Or as Maxwell put it: 'the system left to itself in its actual state of motion will, sooner or later, pass through every phase which is consistent with the equation of energy.' This assumption, proof of which eluded several generations of mathematicians, is at the root of Maxwell's and Boltzmann's development of the kinetic theory. *On Boltzmann's Theorem* is one of Maxwell's most formidable contributions to modern science; it is the foundation of statistical mechanics – a subject which has allowed physicists to deal elegantly with large quantities of molecules and the resulting bulk properties of matter in all its forms.

These two masterful works display the full brilliance of Maxwell's mature scientific talents. They may not be as revolutionary as his theory of electromagnetism; but they are technically scintillating.

In the mid 1870s Maxwell's capacity for work seemed inexhaustible. To his research, book-writing, lecturing and directing the Cavendish he added the scientific editorship of the *Encyclopaedia Britannica* and wrote many of the articles of the ninth edition – on Atom, Attraction, Capillarity, Constitution of Bodies, Diagrams, Diffusion, Ether, Faraday, Harmonic Analysis – summarizing a substantial amount of contemporary physics.

Amidst this welter of activity Maxwell resumed writing verse, his vein leaning now to the sardonic. During the 1874 British Association meeting in Belfast he delivered himself of several poems, in one of which he refers to members of this highly respected body in this way:

> So we who sat, oppressed with science,
> As British asses, wise and grave . . .

And after hearing a lecture by Tait in 1876:

> Ye British Asses, who expect to hear
> Ever some new thing,
> I've nothing to tell, but what, I fear,
> May be a true thing.
> For Tait comes with his plummet and his line,
> Quick to detect your
> Old bosh new dressed in what you call a fine
> Popular lecture.

An interesting reflection on Maxwell's attitude towards science is that, in an age of intense industrialization and technical optimism, he stayed aloof from technology. With his experimental flair, his great physical insight, and his reputation, he should have been much in demand. And indeed he was commanded in 1876 to appear before the Queen – to explain to her, among other things, the importance of a vacuum and of Crookes' radiometer. He described the experience in a letter to his uncle R. D. Cay:

> I was sent for to London, to be ready to explain to the Queen why Otto von Guericke devoted himself to the discovery of nothing, and to show her the two hemispheres in which he kept it, and the pictures of the 16 horses who could not separate the hemispheres and how after 200 years W. Crookes has come much nearer to nothing and has sealed it up in a glass globe for public inspection. Her Majesty however let us off very easily and did not make much ado about nothing, as she had much heavy work cut out for her all the rest of the day.

Maxwell perhaps was simply too busy – or, what amounts to the same thing, insufficiently motivated – to delve into technology. Yet in the abstract his interest in contemporary developments was lively enough. After the 1876 invention of the telephone in the U. S. A. he devoted his entertaining 1878 Rede lecture to it. In this, perhaps the most charming of his public lectures, he mocks, in passing, evolutionists such as Herbert Spencer:

> One great beauty of Professor Bell's invention is that the instruments at the two ends of the line are precisely alike . . . The perfect symmetry of the whole apparatus – the wire in the middle, the two telephones at the ends of the wire; and the two gossips at the ends of the telephones, may be very fascinating to a mere mathematician, but it would not satisfy the evolutionist of the Spenserain type, who would consider anything with both ends alike, such as the Amphisbaena, or Mr Bright's terrier, or Mr Bell's telephone, to be an organism of a very low type, which must have its functions differentiated before any satisfactory integration can take place.

During these years Maxwell also wrote a number of book reviews, in which at times he exhibits an exceptionally fine touch. It seems difficult to conceive, for instance, that a serious review of a technical book could be either poetic or touching; yet Maxwell infuses both qualities into a piece written for *Nature* in 1874. This was a review of a book by the well-known Belgian physicist and mathematician Plateau, which had appeared under the forbidding title of *Experimental and Theoretical Statics of Liquids Subjected solely to Molecular Forces* – primarily a study of thin liquid films, like those observed in the blowing of soap bubbles, which the author used as illustrations. And so Maxwell entitles his review simply *Plateau on Soap Bubbles* and begins it in this manner:

> On an Etruscan vase in the Louvre figures of children are seen blowing bubbles. These children probably enjoyed their occupation just as modern children do. Our admiration of the beautiful and delicate forms, growing and developing themselves, the feeling that it is *our* breath which is turning dirty soap-suds into spheres of splendour, the fear least by irreverent touch we may cause the gorgeous vision to vanish with a sputter of soapy water in our eyes, our wistful gaze as we watch the perfect bubble when it sails away from the pipe's mouth to join, somewhere in the sky, all the other beautiful things that have vanished before it, assure us that, whatever our nominal age may be we are of the same family as those Etruscan children. . . .

At this stage of his busy life Maxwell was further burdened by the poor health of his wife. The origin and nature of her illness are not clear. From passing references in his correspondence it is known that by 1875 he was often worried and frequently nursed her himself. On one occasion he did not sleep in a bed for three weeks, dozing the nights away in a chair by Katherine's bedside – yet he spent the days at the Cavendish, carrying on his work as usual, seemingly unruffled, his energies unimpaired. It has been suggested that Mrs Maxwell's illness was primarily hysterical in origin; but of course we cannot be sure. She was, it is certain, not popular with her husband's students, colleagues, or their wives. One student is quoted by Whittaker as referring to Maxwell's 'terrible wife' and Mrs J. J. Thomson has stated that 'She was, to put it bluntly, a difficult woman.' Given the environment and the gentility of the times, these were strong words. However, little that is relevant to this has ever been committed to writing. There is a story that, at an evening gathering in Cambridge, Mrs Maxwell told her husband with some acerbity: 'James, you're beginning to enjoy yourself; it is time we go home.' It has been said also that she was rude to Maxwell's colleagues; that she preferred to lead the life of the country gentry to which she felt entitled, that she attempted to interfere with her husband's work. Some of these allegations stem from suspect sources – such as Mrs Tait who, it has been claimed, was jealous of Maxwell's brilliance. It is, in short, difficult to disentangle truth from malicious academic gossip. But whatever the reason, Katherine Maxwell seems to have generated a fair measure of ill-will amongst her husband's colleagues.

The details of the Maxwell's married life may never be available to us. This is a pity, for they would have shed further light on James Clerk Maxwell. In the early and mid-1870s he was at the peak of his powers; she, an invalid. On his part there was real affection and, no doubt, an element of duty. They were childless. Passion, one suspects, played a secondary – if any – role in their relationship. When Maxwell travelled or was for any reason separated from his wife, he wrote to her regularly, telling her tales of the university or of his relationships with his colleagues. There is, in those letters, the usual impress of Christian piety. Thus in December 1873:

> I am always with you in spirit, but there is One who is nearer to you and to me than we ever can be to each other, and it is only through Him and in Him that we can ever really get to know each other. Let us try to realise the great mystery in Ephesians v, and then we shall be in the right position with respect to the world outside, the men and women whom Christ came to save from their sins.

Ephesians v contains some of St Paul's more horrendous moral thunder – being an admonition to all against fornication and to wives to 'be subject to your husbands as to the Lord; for the man is the head of the woman, just as Christ is the head of the church'. The great mystery Maxwell refers to is perhaps the reference therein to the words of the Scripture that 'a man shall leave his father and mother and shall be joined to his wife, and the two shall become one flesh'. Whether Katherine found all this edifying is difficult to tell.

There are some photographs of Katherine, taken about 1868–70. There is about her a vaguely unsettled aura – a mixture of resignation, piety, and perhaps a touch of aggravation – an aura she maintains posing with or without her husband. In the picture of them together Maxwell looks not so much tired as subdued; there is a streak of grey in his beard, and his hairline is receding. There is a contrived feel about this photograph – the painted scenery, the slightly absurd dog, Katherine's expression. This, sadly, is the only objective record of a moment in Maxwell's private life.

Maxwell's health was good until 1876 or 1877. His hair by then was iron grey, but his figure remained sturdy and his step elastic. He walked everyday from his house on Scroope Terrace to the Cavendish, accompanied by his dog Tobi. A contemporary describes him at work in the laboratory:

> In performing his private experiments at the laboratory, Maxwell was very neat-handed and expeditious. When working thus, or when thinking about a problem, he had a habit of whistling, not loudly, but in a half-subdued manner, no particular tune discernible, but a sort of running accompaniment to his inward thoughts . . . He could carry the full strength of his mental faculties rapidly from one subject to another, and could pursue his studies under distractions which most students would find intolerable, such as a loud conversation in the room where he was at work. On these occasions he used, in a manner, to take his dog into his confidence, and would say softly, 'Tobi, Tobi', at intervals, and after thinking and working for a time, would at last say (for example), 'It must be so; Plato (i.e. Plateau), thou reasonest well.' He would then join in the conversation.

He remained in all respects as he had always been – an eccentric in manners and speech, occasionally inarticulate and difficult to follow. Another Cambridge friend, F. J. A. Hort, put it this way:

> The old peculiarities of his manner of speaking remained virtually unchanged. It was still no easy matter to read the course of his thoughts through the humorous veil which they wove for themselves; and still the obscurity would now and then be lit up by some radiant explosion.

Even now, as a celebrated Cambridge professor, Maxwell could, if ill at ease, lapse into a condition verging on incoherence. Thus a Fellow of King's College, Cambridge, having consulted Maxwell about a lightning rod for the chapel, reported that the great man's spoken explanations were chaotic and unintelligible – but that he left written instructions which were perfectly lucid.

Maxwell's activities – scientific, literary or administrative – were by then extraordinarily diverse; not even he could have been able to pursue all the avenues of work and ideas that came his way. That he experienced frustration is clear from the account Campbell gives of their meeting in 1877. They had been discussing Maxwell's editorship of Cavendish's electrical researches:

> he took the MS of this book out of a cabinet, and began showing it to me and discoursing about it in the old eager, playful, affectionate way, just as with the magic discs in boyhood, or the register of the colour-box observations at a later time, in the little study at Glenlair. 'And what', I said, 'of your investigations in various ways?' 'I have to give up so many things,' he answered, with a sad look, which till then I had never seen in his eyes. Even before this, as it now appears, he had felt the first symptoms of the inexorable malady, which in the spring of 1879 assumed a dangerous aspect, and killed him in the autumn of that year.

It is sad that after Aberdeen we know so little of Maxwell's private life. His youth is well documented, thanks to Campbell. But concerning his private yearnings in later life, his passions, his dissatisfactions, angers, ecstasies, frustrations – all that goes into making a human being – our information is tantalizingly sparse. To some extent this is due to his friend's excessive discretion. In part, though, it is Maxwell's own doing: he was an intensely private person. Until recently scientists have not been prone to write their memoirs. One recalls how, at the age of sixty-seven, Einstein was asked to produce a brief auto-biography and responded with an essay on the recent history of physics and of the special and general theories of relativity, excusing himself with these words: 'the essential in the being of a man of my type lies precisely in *what* he thinks and *how* he thinks.' Maxwell's comments on autobiography, at the age of twenty-five, were pungent: 'The stomach-pump of the con-fessional ought only to be used in cases of manifest poisoning. More gentle remedies are better for the constitution in ordinary cases.' And there is also the ultimate fact that great men and women of science have usually been too busy to write auto-biographies or keep personal diaries. Notwithstanding, most of us have an understandable curiosity about our great scientists. Their ideas are not enough; we want to see Einstein, Newton or Maxwell as men, not merely as purveyors of theories – no matter how splendid.

Maxwell's letters, poems and essays show that his life had many strands, all important to him, all running deep – religion, philosophy, love of family, a sense of duty to his fellow men and women. But science provided the day-by-day *framework* within which he ordered his existence, evolved and thought. All his activities were linked: he was strikingly *whole*. His life is full of interesting continuities. A childhood fascination with contrivances, with bell-ringers, with the play of light – these grade into adolescent scientific experiments and musings and, almost imperceptibly, into serious, brilliant and ultimately revolutionary work in mechanics, colour theory and electro-magnetism. An early sense of wonder and love of nature never left him and, broadening as the years went by, led to an appreciation of philosophy unique amongst his scientific con-temporaries, which gave his work on electricity and magnetism its depth. The love of philosophy was linked to a streak of mysticism which found expression in what was, by virtue of his upbringing and early environment, the only avenue open to him – a traditional Christian faith. From this stem his social views; archaic as they seem to us, they were well meant and part of a coherent *Weltanschauung*. It was all of one piece.

Maxwell had innate gifts – a marvellous geometrical imagination, an unusually fine memory, an ability to write – and qualities such as humour and kindness. Nevertheless, except for those who knew him well, he was a difficult man to feel close to. His Calvinism would have been trying to those not sharing it. His attitudes towards society were feudal. It is true that these were tempered by compassion – he gave time to working men's lectures, as well as to his Glenlair tenants. But he must have often found himself out of sympathy with some of his more interesting contemporaries; there is no record of his having sought the company of men like Darwin, Huxley or Spencer. His poor record as a teacher suggests a lack of empathy for others' intellectual difficulties. His humour, usually gentle, could turn biting. Some of his railleries were fairly savage and must have hurt their recipients – such as John Alexander Frere 'the small man who lived sincere'. His references to Osborne Reynolds were harsh – although this unfortunate affair is best treated as an aberration, a consequence of the terminal and painful illness from which he was suffering at the time (such certainly was the attitude of his friends); Maxwell was neither vain nor ambitious, and it was not in his nature to be petty.

The professional attitudes Maxwell admired most in others suggest the attributes he himself would have liked to be remembered by. In a commemorative article on Faraday he wrote:

> It is to be hoped that the nobleness of his simple, undramatic life, will live long in men's memories as the discoveries which have immortalised his name. Here was no hunger after popular applause, no jealousy of other men's work, no swerving from the well-beloved, self-imposed task of 'working, finishing, publishing'.

As he grew older, Maxwell's commitment to science became even more intense, his time more fully taken up by professional activities, his correspondence wholly scientific – even his poems dealt with science. Psychologists often point out that great scientists' total engagement in their work tends to go hand in hand with a rejection of other things – that they are escaping into worlds of their own creation, worlds they can master and control. Such analyses are most naturally applied to theoretical physicists – builders, so to speak, of their own universes. And this can be argued persuasively enough for men like Einstein, who revelled in solitude – 'I live in that solitude which is painful in youth, but delicious in the years of maturity' – or Maxwell – who, by his own admission, had better understanding of things than people: 'My interest is always in things rather than in persons' said he to Hort shortly before his death. Yet it is hard to avoid feeling that these psychological 'escape' theories are too facile. They devalue some of mankind's finest intellectual and spiritual instincts – his philosophical, metaphysical or religious thirsts, call them what you will.

Characteristic of Maxwell's interest in science are its philosophical and metaphysical underpinnings. In this again he reminds one of Einstein who was not only deeply concerned with epistemological questions, but was also something of a mystic – often bringing God into his arguments: 'God does not play dice', said he when attacking the philosophical base of quantum mechanics, or 'God is subtle, but he is not malicious' and 'I want to know how God created this world. I am not interested in this or that phenomenon, in the spectrum of this or that element. I want to know His thoughts, the rest are details.' Maxwell is more traditional, and certainly more modest when he says:

> Teach me so Thy works to read
> That my faith – new strength accruing –
> May from world to world proceed,

Wisdom's fruitful search pursuing;
Till, thy truth my mind imbuing,
I proclaim the Eternal Creed,
Oft the glorious theme renewing
God our Lord is God indeed.

Unlike Einstein, Maxwell is not above using the lessons of science to bolster his religious views – as in his 1872 British Association lecture in which, referring to molecules, he concludes:

> They continue this day as they were created – perfect in number and measure and weight, and from the ineffaceable characters impressed upon them we may learn that those aspirations after accuracy in measurement, truth and statement, and justice in action, which we reckon among our noblest attributes as men, are ours because they are essential constituents of the image of Him who in the beginning created, not only the heaven and the earth, but the material of which heaven and earth consist.

Maxwell, of course, had no way of knowing that molecules or atoms are neither permanent nor ultimate constituents of matter. It is always risky to mix faith with fact – even when you are James Clerk Maxwell. Nevertheless, the metaphysical foundation of his interest in the universe is a timeless one. It had motivated Pythagoras and Newton before him and Einstein, soon after, was moved by a similar, if less traditional, vein of mysticism.

Maxwell's importance in the history of scientific thought is comparable to Einstein's (whom he inspired) and to Newton's (whose influence he curtailed). All three men had the rare distinction, as theoretical physicists, of significantly altering the way in which we see the world – a distinction shared by only a handful of scientists since the Renaissance: Copernicus, Kepler, Galileo, Newton, Faraday and Darwin come to mind. Comparisons between such great figures are dangerous. Yet one cannot fail to be struck by certain similarities in outlook between Maxwell and Einstein. Neither was a formalist – their strength lay not in mathematical ability, but in a formidable physical insight. Neither was a specialist; their knowledge of physics was broad and all-encompassing, issuing from a clear vision of what was important. Both men were highly intuitive, willing to take logical jumps which made lesser men shudder. And both were fundamentally philosophers – natural philosophers, to use the fitting nineteenth century label. Their interest accordingly lay in science as knowledge rather than in its applications. In this, as in much else, they were out of step with their times.

Throughout history prevailing attitudes towards science have changed and shifted. Science's prehistoric roots lie in a mixture of practical and religious concerns. In ancient Greece, where *pure* science and mathematics were born, the primary motive for exploring the world was philosophical (even Archimedes, that most *applied* of Greek natural philosophers, was somewhat contemptuous of his practical endeavours). The Greek commitment was to knowledge, rather than power. As Western science developed – after the Renaissance – the pendulum swung back. Knowledge *was* power. In Maxwell's time, the pursuit of knowledge *qua* power was strongly in the ascendant. The industrial revolution was the embodiment of this view – an ethos which was culminated in today's huge industrial and military technologies. Major nineteenth century social philosophers and economists such as Marx saw science as a *tool* for the fulfilment of socio-economic needs – a view implicitly accepted today by marxists and capitalists alike. There can be little doubt that science and technology – knowledge and power – are in some sense necessary and complementary to each other. Yet the greatest figures in science, men of genius like Newton, Maxwell, Faraday or Einstein had little interest in the power aspect of the equation: they left its pursuit, i.e. the applications of science, to others. They were well aware of the practical possibilities in their work – they could not help but be. Faraday said it all in his classic rejoinder to a question concerning the *use* of his discovery of induction:

'What use is a baby?'. One remembers too how Einstein, during World War II, volunteered to work for the U.S. Office of Naval Research. Nevertheless the intellectual commitment of an Einstein, a Faraday, or a Maxwell to technology and the pursuit of power inherent in knowledge was slight or non-existent. The picture sometimes painted of our great men as devoting their lives to 'the service of mankind' is in fact largely fraudulent. Men of genius have their own, independent, private, essentially anarchic wellsprings which need not be consonant with those of the society they live in. Maxwell's motivations were philosophical and metaphysical; in this he was out of the mainstream of his society and somewhat of a maverick amongst his contemporaries.

There are thus many reasons why Maxwell was not fully appreciated during his lifetime. The revolution he had wrought was too deep for his scientific friends – people who, on the whole, lacked the philosophical sophistication to abandon their mechanistic world view. And he was out of tune with the society he lived in; unlike his friend W. Thomson, he had little wish to involve himself in technological developments. His metaphysical interests, not to mention his Calvinism, also kept him from establishing close ties outside a small circle of like-minded people. Add to this that he was an immensely busy and highly private person, and it is not surprising that his public image was less brilliant than that of some of his contemporaries. Certainly he obtained less recognition than Faraday, or than W. Thomson who was knighted in 1866, became Lord Kelvin of Largs in 1892 and was buried in Westminster Abbey, or than G. G. Stokes (knighted in 1889). Less easy to understand is the fact that Maxwell's image is still rather faint today – if not among physicists, then at least among lay people. It seems odd, for instance, that the Queen's speech at the Royal Society's 1960 tricentenary celebration, listing a number of famous fellows of the Society, makes no mention of James Clerk Maxwell.

A Canadian physicist, G. MacDonald, who visited the scene

of young Maxwell's tribulations at the Edinburgh Academy, was taken aback at the casual way in which his memory was treated there. The Edinburgh Academy *Chronicle* of June–July 1931 did carry a centenary piece about him, but the general effect was somewhat marred by a rhetorical question towards the end of the article: 'Now, was Maxwell a very great man – or only a great man?'

An amusing tale – related by R. V. Jones – illustrating Maxwell's uncertain fame goes back to a public meeting in Aberdeen on 28 August 1857, at which it was decided that the town had no suitable hall for the main meeting of the British Association planned for 1859. It was agreed to raise the money by public subscription and build one; the resulting edifice eventually became the Music Hall. The shareholders, amongst whom was Maxwell, received small dividends for many years thereafter, paid out by a local firm of advocates. These payments continued for many years and in 1920 an advertisement appeared in the Aberdeen newspapers inquiring whether anyone knew the whereabouts of one James Clerk Maxwell. There was in Aberdeen at least one man who both read the local papers and knew who Maxwell was – a school inspector, who promptly went to the advocates and said to the head of the firm: 'Do you really mean to tell me that you've never heard of James Clerk Maxwell, the most famous man to ever walk the streets of Aberdeen?' 'No,' said the advocate, 'who was he?' The inspector explained, and the man listened. 'This is very interesting indeed,' said the advocate, 'let me tell you why we published the advertisement. For years we've been sending dividends arising from the Music Hall addressed to 'Mr James Clerk Maxwell, Marischal College', but we have always had them returned 'Not known'.

12

THE LAST ACT

The philosopher Fichte once said: 'What is called death cannot break up my work; because my work must be accomplished, because I have to fulfil my vocation, there is no limit to my life. I am eternal.' Maxwell's work is, in Fichte's sense, eternal – a keystone to our understanding of the universe, it transcends time.

Maxwell's own views on eternity were of a piece with his traditional religious creed. He believed staunchly in the Christian concept of the immortal soul; about this he had no doubts. He died as he had lived, his death an integral element of the whole that was his life – his last and inevitable act on earth, to be carried out with grace, humour and faith.

The first signs of ill-health, early warnings that all was not well, came in the spring of 1877, when Maxwell developed heartburn and a difficulty in digesting meat. He resorted to bicarbonate of soda, which seemed to help. For a while, life went on as before. Maxwell wrote his scientific papers, his reviews and lectures, ran the Cavendish and worried about Katherine far more than about himself. For almost two years his energies seemed unimpaired; he would have had little inkling of the seriousness of his illness. But dyspeptic symptoms kept recurring; the effectiveness of the bicarbonate decreased; slowly he got worse. In December 1878, blaming overwork, he begged out of writing a contribution for Huxley's project 'English Men of Science'.

By April 1879 he had difficulty swallowing and was in pain, and mentioned his symptoms to Dr Paget – the Maxwell's Cambridge physician – in a letter dealing chiefly with Katherine's health. His illness was now sapping his strength and impairing his concentration. During the Easter term he was able to do little but attend to his lectures and make daily fleeting visits to the laboratory. Returning to Glenlair in June, he attempted to write a review of W. K. Clifford's *Lectures and Essays*. This was a difficult task. Clifford had died in March. While disagreeing with him on many issues, Maxwell had liked him: 'there were many things in the book that needed trouncing, and yet the trouncing had to be done with extreme care and gentleness, Clifford was such a nice fellow.' Maxwell's mind, however, refused the work – he could no longer concentrate. He understood then that he was seriously ill. He was, in fact, suffering from the same form of abdominal cancer which had killed his mother.

On 21 August he wrote to Stokes – a letter dealing largely with the proofs of his last great paper *On Stresses in Rarefied Gases*:

> My Dear Stokes,
>   I have not been able for work of any kind for some time, so that it is with difficulty that I can answer your letter, though it is about my own paper, and you have been taking so much trouble to make it somewhat like a paper . . .

Following a list of minor corrections for the proofs, he concludes:

> I hope the R. S. will not send me any papers to report on for I could not do it.
> My wife got caught in the rain on the 13th, and on Monday I was afraid of bronchitis, but the doctor thinks that it has taken a better turn now, but she is very much distressed with neuralgia in the face with toothache. She was much pleased by getting a letter from Mrs Stokes this morning.

Among the subscribers to Dr Smith's Optics, 1738, appears the name of 'Mr Gabriel Stocks.' I dare say however your optical studies were already somewhat advanced (from a heredity point of view) in 1738.
Yours very truly,

J. Clerk Maxwell

A week later he wrote a missive to Tait, which he entitled *Headstone in Search of a New Sensation*:

While meditating, as is my wont on a Saturday afternoon, on the enjoyments and employments which might serve to occupy one or two of the aeonian and aetherial phases of existence to which I am looking forward, I began to be painfully conscious of the essentially finite variety of the sensations which can be elicited by the combined action of a finite number of nerves, whether these nerves are of a protoplasmic or eschatoplasmic nature . . .

The rest of this letter – his last one to Tait – is a brave but rambling effort at humour, ending with the admission:

I have been so seedy that I could not read anything however profound without going to sleep over it.

dp/dt.

Yet at this stage Maxwell's failing energies still had periods of renewal for, during that summer, he was involved in his argument with Reynolds – an argument leading to an exchange of letters between Maxwell, Reynolds, Stokes and Thomson (who acted as the second referee). Maxwell's scathing remarks on Reynolds ('an acrobat who drives 24 in hand . . . ') were contained, as we have seen, in a letter addressed to Stokes dated September. That illness had affected his equanimity is most likely. Tait, writing to Stokes in December, stated that in his opinion 'Maxwell's hereditary malady had begun to affect him some months before his death . . . I began to fear that his mind was affected; but, happily, this phase was very transient'. Tait was referring here not so much to the Reynolds incident as to the fact that Maxwell had at the time independently recommended two men – Chrystal and Garnett – for one job: the Edinburgh Chair of Mathematics. A difficult professional controversy, correcting proofs, writing recommendations affecting other people's careers, whilst in the throes of terminal cancer would have taxed the sanity of any man.

In September Maxwell still had the strength to receive at Glenlair his assistant William Garnett and Mrs Garnett. When on arrival their host emerged to greet them on the steps of the house, Garnett was shocked at his appearance. For several days Maxwell put on a brave show for his guests, entertaining them with conversation, bringing out family souvenirs for inspection, including the celebrated – and inevitable – bagpipes Captain James Clerk had used to stay afloat after his shipwreck. However, Maxwell could not ride with the Garnetts in his carriage because the shaking caused him too much pain.

On 2 October Maxwell was told by Dr Sanders of Edinburgh that he had not more than a month to live. He took this with a calm and self-control which amazed the local physician – Dr Lorraine of Castle Douglas – who, in a letter to Dr Paget, described Maxwell with quite unworkaday admiration as 'a perfect example of a Christian gentleman.'

On 3 October Katherine Maxwell wrote to Mrs Stokes. She makes no mention of the devastating news, saying only:

> My Dear Mrs Stokes,
>
> We had 3 Doctors yesterday and they all agreed on one thing, that Mr Maxwell must go at once to Dr Paget, who is celebrated in what they think this complaint. Dr Saunders I liked very much. We hope to leave to-day, when we can have an invalid carriage to go direct to Cambridge without stopping anywhere. Wonderful from being so weak all summer I can do everything, order the packing &c. With kindest regards to you all,
>
> Ever yr affecte
K. M. Clerk Maxwell
>
> We will likely leave for Cambridge Monday.

In Maxwell's handwriting:

> A small but heavy box arrived this morning from Cambridge directed to Arthur. We shall take it back to Cambridge, as Arthur will probably be soon back at King's.
>
> I am a little stronger to-day.

It is possible that Maxwell chose to hide from Katherine the fact that he was dying. Even so it was obvious to all that he was gravely ill and it is peculiar, to say the least, to find Katherine commenting here on how well she feels. To have Maxwell worrying about the belongings of Stokes' son Arthur is almost equally astonishing.

Upon arriving in Cambridge on 8 October, Maxwell was very weak and in great pain – some of which Dr Paget managed to relieve. Little else, however, could be done for him. Dr Paget recalls Maxwell's last weeks in these words:

In Cambridge his more severe sufferings were gradually in great measure relieved, but the disease continued its progress. It was the disease of which his mother had died at the same age.

As he had been in health, so was he in sickness and in the face of death. The calmness of his mind was never once disturbed. His sufferings were acute for some days after his return to Cambridge, and, even after mitigation, were still of a kind to try severely any ordinary patience and fortitude. But they were never spoken of by him in a complaining tone. In the midst of them his thoughts and considerations were rather for others than for himself.

Neither did the approach of death disturb his habitual composure. Before leaving Glenlair he had learnt from Prof. Sanders that he had not more than about a month to live. A few days before his death he asked me how much longer he could last. The inquiry was made with the most perfect calmness. He wished to live until the expected arrival from Edinburgh of his friend and relative Mr Colin Mackenzie. His only anxiety seemed to be about his wife, whose health had for a few years been delicate, and had recently become worse . . .

His intellect also remained clear and apparently unimpaired to the last. While his bodily strength was ebbing away to death, his mind never once wandered or wavered, but remained clear to the very end. No man ever met death more consciously or more calmly.

Shortly before the end Maxwell confided to Dr Hort:

I have been thinking how very gently I have always been dealt with. I have never had a violent shove all my life. The only desire which I can have is like David to serve my own generation by the will of God, and then fall asleep.

169

He died as he had lived – with grace, composure and dignity. Present by him on the 5th of November were Katherine and Colin Mackenzie, who left this description of Maxwell's last moments:

> A few minutes before his death, Professor Clerk Maxwell was being held up in bed, struggling for breath, when he said slowly and distinctly, 'God help me! God help my wife!' He turned to me and said, 'Colin, you are strong, lift me up;' He next said, 'Lay me down lower, for I am very low myself, and it suits me to lie low.' After this he breathed deeply and slowly and, with a long look at his wife, passed away.

★   ★   ★

In the Peterhouse College library in Cambridge there is a letter from Katherine Clerk Maxwell to Mrs Elizabeth Dunn of Bath – the Lizzie of Maxwell's youth. Dated 26 May, it is addressed to 'My dear Lizzy' and thanks her for her 'sweet letter', and enquires solicitously of her daughter Ella.

Katherine died in 1886. Glenlair passed to the Wedderburns. Over the years the land was sold off. John Wedderburn-Maxwell, a military man, owned it in 1929 when the big house burned down. It was never repaired and now stands a gaping, forlorn ruin, assaulted by the elements, slowly crumbling amidst the remains of its grounds.

Near the village of Parton in Galloway there is a small cemetery – three acres or so of meadow, surrounded by low stone walls. The grass, tight and close-cropped, is springy underfoot; a few tall pines and oaks provide a scatter of shade; moss and lichen nibble at the weathered tombs. In the middle stands the kirk, a heavy, sombre building of dark slate and red sandstone, with high latticed windows and a square, solid, east-facing belfry. By it are the ruins of an ancient chapel – four walls and a gable, roofless, open to the sky. Scattered around this are graves – slabs of old red sandstone, some barely showing above ground, others large and massive, some standing or leaning, others lying, their inscriptions mostly illegible, worn by centuries of wind, rain, and frost.

I came here one bright day in early spring, with the sunlight playing on the red-brown tombstones and snowdrops dotting the grass amidst the rough slabs, the celtic crosses and *memento mori*. To the west sprawled the River Dee, a blue stretch at the foot of yellowing, patchily wooded hills. High in the north were the Rhinns of Kells – immaculately white, snow-blanketed still by the last of the winter storms. I came looking for the grave of James Clerk Maxwell, and found it within the old chapel walls. The headstone was of polished granite and bore four names: John Clerk Maxwell and his wife Frances Cay, their son James and his wife Katherine Mary. Two complete generations lay here below the ruined north wall, under one headstone. Looking down on them from a small earthen dais – the old altar – were two more graves, the only others in the chapel, belonging clearly to persons of some local standing. The Clerk Maxwells had been an unpretentious, close-knit family; and so they remained in death.

BIBLIOGRAPHY

Biographies of great men and women of science are bedevilled by one particular difficulty: most of the material relating to their work is highly technical. This is not to imply that the contributions to human thought of an Einstein, a Newton, or a Maxwell are beyond the ken of persons untrained in science – not at all. In the appreciation of science, the differences between the non-scientist and the scientist are analogous to the relationships of the art-lover and the artist. One does not have to be a painter to appreciate Michelangelo. Neither does one need training in science to understand and enjoy the import of a properly explained scientific theory; popular myths to the contrary, this requires no special 'scientific bent' – merely a sufficient level of interest. But it presupposes a real effort on the part of scientists to explain their field in non-technical terms – an effort which, to be quite honest, is not always made.

It is only recently that sustained attention has been given by scientists to explain Maxwell's ideas to the lay person. In the following bibliography I have listed several such efforts – my objective being to offer the general reader a choice of further material not requiring a high level of technical training. I have classified my references by content – as biographical, as discussing Maxwell's ideas, or primarily as background material.

When the material referred to is rather technical or difficult, I indicate as much.

Biographical material

Lewis Campbell and W. Garnett, *The Life of James Clerk Maxwell*, London 1882 (there is a second edition (1884) containing a few additional letters but no poems). Long out of print, this book is hard to find although most major libraries should have it. It is a gold mine of Maxwell correspondence and of information concerning his life, particularly of his younger years. Its reverential tone, which can be irritating, makes it difficult to see the man behind Campbell's portrait of him, but the abundance of correspondence and Maxwell writings reproduced in *The Life* makes up for much of this. There are, however, important gaps. There is hardly any material on Katherine; this is unfortunate because most stories told of her by Maxwell's colleagues or their wives are not flattering. Campbell, of course, could not have said anything unfavourable about her, even had he wanted to do so – she was still alive when he wrote his biography. But the fact that he says very little about her may itself be significant; after all, had he thought highly of his great friend's wife, he would have made it clear. Also, whether from Victorian discretion or because of Katherine, Campbell never so much as hints at Maxwell's youthful feelings for Elizabeth Cay, and we have to wait until 1975 to find C. W. F. Everitt unearthing this affair in print. *The Life* is the source of the Maxwell poetry and of much of the correspondence I have quoted in chapters 4, 5, 7, 8, 10, 11, and 12. Like all other Maxwell biographers and essayists I am glad to acknowledge my indebtedness to Lewis Campbell.

J. G. Crowther, *British Scientists of the Nineteenth Century*, London 1935. Like most of Crowther's writings on science, the chapter on Maxwell is entertaining and interesting. In places, however, it lapses into speculation. Thus there appears to be little evidence for the suggestion that Maxwell's arduous work on Saturn's rings was a conscious intellectual tactic designed to establish himself first as a master technician, before offering up his more controversial electromagnetic ideas to his colleagues.

C. Domb, *James Clerk Maxwell in London 1860–1865*, Notes and Records of the Royal Society of London (1980) vol. 35, no. 1, pp. 67–103. Of all available literature on Maxwell, this carefully researched article gives the most thorough account of Maxwell's life and work during this period. In particular it explodes the myth that Maxwell was *asked* to resign from King's

College on account of his poor performance as a teacher. I am indebted to Professor Domb's article not only for information covering the London years, but also for the account of Maxwell's unsuccessful attempt in 1868 to obtain the principalship of St Andrews.

C. W. F. Everitt, *James Clerk Maxwell, Physicist and Natural Philosopher*, New York 1975. A brief but carefully written biographical section contains the first mention of the *affaire* Elizabeth Cay (*Lizzie*). Everitt obtained a certain amount of information on this from Miss E. W. Dunn (Elizabeth's daughter from her marriage to a Mr Dunn of Bath), shortly before she died in her nineties. Everitt, it seems, is the only Maxwell scholar to have interviewed her. He believes that Katherine Maxwell was jealous of Elizabeth and that furthermore, to use his words, the Cays *contempt* for her 'cannot have helped'. The cool relationships with the Cays must however have been largely confined to the female side of the Cay family, for after the marriage Charles and William remained frequent visitors at Glenlair, and Maxwell maintained a steady, albeit largely business correspondence with his uncle Robert. These can be found in the Peterhouse archives, Cambridge.

R. V. Jones, *The Complete Physicist: James Clerk Maxwell 1831–1879*, Yearbook of the Royal Society of Edinburgh (1980) pp. 5–23. Offers some amusing insights into Maxwell's Aberdeen period. This article is the source of my information regarding the manner of Maxwell's dismissal from Aberdeen and also of the anecdote concluding chapter 11.

C. G. Knott, *Life and Scientific Work of P. G. Tait*, Cambridge 1911. Written, like Campbell's *The Life*, in the Victorian hagiographic mode, it is not an easy read. A student of Tait's, Knott clearly venerated his teacher and goes to some pains to explain why. The book is well worth dipping into both for information on Tait's relationship with Maxwell and for an inside view on nineteenth century physics. It contains the full text of Maxwell's last letter to Tait mentioned in chapter 12.

J. Larmor, ed. *Memoir and Scientific Correspondence of Sir George Gabriel Stokes*, 2 vols, London 1910. Contains a number of letters to and from Maxwell, including Katherine Maxwell's letter to Mrs Stokes quoted in chapter 12; D. K. C. Macdonald, *Faraday, Maxwell and Kelvin*, London 1965. Within the covers of a thin paperback, three very abbreviated biographies. MacDonald explains quite clearly the relative roles of these three great men in the history of nineteenth century physics; P. G. Tait, *Obituary Notice of Clerk Maxwell*, Proc.Roy.Soc.Ed., 1879, x, p. 332. The information contained here will also be found in Campbell's *The Life*;

J. J. Thomson, ed. *James Clerk Maxwell 1831–1879*, Cambridge 1931. This centenary volume contains a series of tributes by twentieth century physicists. A number of personal reminiscences by Sir Horace Lamb, Sir Ambrose Fleming, J. J. Thomson and others are of some biographical interest.

Maxwell's science and ideas

In the original, Maxwell's technical writing is largely inaccessible to the non-scientist – who has to rely upon second-hand accounts and analyses. The following is an incomplete list which the 'general reader' may find helpful.

Stephen Brush, *The Kind of Motion We Call Heat*, Amsterdam 1976. While this book gives useful insight into the kinetic theory of gases, it also supplies a detailed account of the Maxwell-Reynolds confrontation; J. G. Crowther, *loc. cit.*, offers a highly readable summary of Maxwell's scientific work and accomplishments; C. Domb, *James Clerk Maxwell – 100 years later*, Nature, vol. 282, 15 November 1979, pp. 253–9. Written to commemorate the centenary of Maxwell's death, this is a compact and authoritative overview of his work and life.

Albert Einstein, *Out of My Later Years*, New York 1967. Einstein's writings, both technical and popular, are full of references to Maxwell – whom, together with Faraday and Newton, he admired above all scientists. The Einstein quote I use in chapter 1 comes from an essay entitled 'The Fundaments (*sic*) of Theoretical Physics'; C. W. F. Everitt, *loc. cit.*, and in *Applied Optics*, 6 (1967), pp. 639–46 gives a very thorough analysis of Maxwell's scientific work. However, it contains considerable technical material and mathematics and is not recommended for those without a scientific training; R. P. Feynman, R. B. Leighton and M. Sands, *Lectures on Physics*, London 1964. While this wholly admirable textbook is designed for physics undergraduates, I thought I should mention it as offering one of the most inspired treatments of electromagnetism available on any level. It is the source of the Feynman quote I have used in chapter 1.

W. Garnett, in Campbell and Garnett's *The Life* (see above) offers a strictly nineteenth century view of Maxwell's work and is thus largely of historical interest – showing how even some of Maxwell's closest collaborators lacked a true perspective on the importance and revolutionary nature of some of his work; P. T. Glazebrook, *James Clerk Maxwell and Modern Physics*, London 1901, is likewise old-fashioned and lacks the necessary perspective; R. V. Jones in *loc. cit.*, and in *Notes Rec. Roy.Soc.Lond.*, 28 (1973), 57–81, offers interesting reflections on Maxwell's scientific ideas. In the former of these articles he describes Maxwell as 'as complete, and as perfect, a physicist as has ever lived' – a view I think most modern physicists would concur with. Whereas I would also agree with his statement that 'Maxwell's conception of the displacement current therefore came from thinking along purely physical lines and not, as is sometimes related in textbooks, by consideration of a missing term in Ampère's circuital relation', it is nevertheless true that there could be no *physical* or logical justification for keeping the concept in the context of a vacuum.

T. S. Kuhn *The Structure of Scientific Revolutions*, Chicago 1970. A classic of the philosophy of science literature, it describes in detail Kuhn's view of the progress of science by periods of crisis and *revolution*, separated by periods of *normal science*. Kuhn provides an interesting discussion of the emergence of the Maxwellian paradigm. However, he says (p. 74) that Maxwell 'still believed his electromagnetic theory compatible with some articulation of the Newtonian mechanical view'. How much is *some*? The quotes from Maxwell's writing which I give suggest that Kuhn may be overstating the case. He goes on to say that: 'Developing a suitable articulation was a challenge to him and his successors'. Yet neither Maxwell's published papers nor his *Treatise on Electricity and Magnetism* show any effort on his part to develop such an articulation, beyond his original vortex model (1862) which he quickly abandoned. W. Thomson, on the other hand, *did* vainly try till the end of his life, but then he never did accept Maxwell's equations as final.

W. D. Niven, ed. *James Clerk Maxwell, Scientific Papers*, 2 vols, Cambridge 1890. With the exception of Maxwell's books, this is most of his scientific *opus*. However, there are omissions: these have been listed by Everitt *loc. cit.* A surprisingly large percentage of these papers is written in a style accessible to people having only a smattering of physics. His other works are *A Treatise on Electricity and Magnetism*, 2 vols, Oxford 1873, also available as a Dover paperback, New York 1954; *Theory of Heat*, London 1870, and many subsequent editions; *Matter and Motion*, London 1877; *Elementary Treatise on Electricity*, W. Garnett, ed. Oxford 1881; revised ed. 1888; and *The Unpublished Electrical Writings of Hon. Henry Cavendish*, Cambridge 1879.

James R. Newman, *James Clerk Maxwell* in *Science and Sensibility*, pp. 139–95, New York 1961. A good essay, but parts of it have mathematical passages which put it out of reach of the general reader.

P. G. Tait, 'Maxwell, James Clerk' in *Encyclopaedia Britannica*, 1954. Appears to be one of the few really enthusiastic endorsements of Maxwell's electromagnetic theory by a British contemporary. Nevertheless, one may be permitted to doubt to what extent Tait fully understood the nature of the revolution wrought by Maxwell. Thus in a lecture in City Hall, Glasgow in 1880 (cf. C. G. Knott, *loc. cit.*) he says of his friend that 'One grand object which he kept before him through his whole scientific life was to reduce electric and magnetic phenomena to mere stresses and motions of the ethereal jelly'. Insofar as his *published* work goes, Maxwell does not in fact seem to have given this particular goal too much attention after 1862. In an article in *Nature*, 29 January 1880, Tait gives a summary of Maxwell's life work. It is here that he states that Maxwell showed him 'the greater part' of a manuscript 'On Faraday's Lines of Force' in 1853.

G. Temple, *Noah's Theorem* – lecture given at Yorkshire Applied Mathematics Colloquium at the University of York, 20 December 1979. It was apparently here that Professor Temple coined this name for Maxwell's fundamental theorem from his *On Hills and Dales*.

R. A. R. Tricker, *The Contributions of Faraday and Maxwell to Electrical Science*, Oxford 1966. Contains a mixture of biographical material, of appraisal and analysis of the work of the two great founders of the electro-magnetic field concept. The non-scientist might well be put off by the presence of numerous equations; but there is a fair amount of general material of a more accessible kind interspersed between the more technical passages. This book is the source of the Cheshire cat grin analogy I mention in chapter 9.

L. C. Woods, 'Maxwell's Models', *Journal of the Institute of Mathematics and its Applications*, vol. 16, January 1980, pp. 11–15. A clear and highly readable analysis of Maxwell's methods of thinking, it also makes some timely points concerning current formalistic tendencies in applied mathematics and theoretical physics. Professor Woods contrasts, in particular, Maxwell's superb use of physical intuition and model-making with modern trends towards often unnecessary formalism. Without doubt this is true; yet the irony is that Maxwell's own inspired espousal of field concepts has led physics into regions of greater abstraction. Parts of this very interesting article will, alas, be tough going for readers untrained in mathematics or science.

General

J. D. Bernal, *Science in History*, 4 vols, London 1965. Bernal's classic contains a great amount of historical material on the evolution of science, from prehistoric to modern times. The interpretation of scientific history offered is obviously coloured by the author's ideology: it is the traditional Marxist view which sees science as a series of responses to socio-economic needs and pressures. Maxwell, nevertheless, is given due prominence – only he and Darwin amongst nineteenth century scientists are given full page portraits – and it is instructive to see how Maxwell's highly individualistic work is accommodated in Bernal's structure: 'The major achievement of the period in physics was the formulation by Maxwell of the *electromagnetic theory of light*. This brought together in one comprehensive theory the results of two generations of experiments and theories in different fields of physics – electricity, magnetism, and optics – and gave them a simple mathematical formulation. Though in itself a triumph of mathematical physics, it depended for its verification on the establishment of accurate units for electricity, a task made necessary by the rise of the electrical industry. In turn, Maxwell's equations were to form the theoretical basis for future electrical engineering, an intricate interplay of theory and practice'. Doctrine, it seems, has risen to the challenge. Yet if the environment in which Maxwell worked reflected these factors, his thought does not seem to have been prey to their influence. There is in great minds a spark of anarchy which is not so easily circumscribed.

G. E. Davie, *The Democratic Intellect – Scotland and her Universities in the Nineteenth Century*, Edinburgh 1961. An interesting account of the Forbes-Hamilton feud and its roots in the broader conflict between Scottish and English educational traditions. The erudite Scottish philosopher lost his battle with Forbes, the Cambridge-educated technician – but not before implanting some very important seeds in young Maxwell's receptive mind.

Paul Feyerabend, *Against Method*, London 1978. Subtitled *Outline of an anarchistic theory of knowledge*, this provocative book maintains that 'Science is an essentially anarchistic enterprise' and that 'The only principle that does not inhibit progress is: *anything goes*'. Maxwell's formulation of electromagnetism is perhaps an example of what Feyerabend has in mind. It could be interesting to try to relate this anarchistic view of the evolution of scientific thought to Jungian views on the role of the subconscious in intellectual creativity – views which, in some measure, Maxwell had adumbrated (see quotes in chapter 7); T. S. Kuhn, *loc. cit.*, offers a different modern view on the manner in which science progresses. It is easier to read than Feyerabend's book and is good background material for anyone wishing to understand the place of scientific revolutions such as Maxwell's in the history of thought.

G. Sarton, *A History of Science*, vols 1 (1952) and 2 (1959), Cambridge, Mass. and G. Sarton, *Introduction to the History of Science*, vols 1–3, Carnegie Institution of Washington, 1927–48. Sarton was an outstanding representative of the old school of science historians, whose impressive erudition was devoted to the careful documenting of the step-by-step progress of human knowledge. These books contain a huge amount of information on ancient and pre-Renaissance science.

E. T. Whittaker, *A History of Theories of the Aether and Electricity*, London 1952. This fluent and beautifully organized book is essential reading for any physicist wishing to understand the early development of electromagnetism until the beginning of the twentieth century. I am much indebted to it in my writing of chapter 9.

Additional bibliographical material

More thorough bibliographies relating to Maxwell's life and thought will be found in Everitt, *loc. cit*; C. Domb in *James Clerk Maxwell in London*; and M. Norton Wise in 'The Mutual Embrace of Electricity and Magnetism', *Science*, 203, 30 March 1979, pp. 1310–18.

INDEX